PENGUIN AFRICAN LIBRARY AP 21

Edited by Ronald Segal

The Development of Modern Nigeria

OKOI ARIKPO

OKOI ARIKPO

The Development of Modern Nigeria

PENGUIN BOOKS

Penguin Books Ltd, Harmondsworth,
Middlesex, England
Penguin Books Inc., 3300 Clipper Mill Road,
Baltimore, Md 21211, U.S.A.
Penguin Books Australia Ltd, Ringwood,
Victoria, Australia

First published by Penguin Books 1967

Made and printed in Great Britain by
Cox & Wyman Ltd, London, Reading and Fakenham
Set in Monotype Plantin

Contents

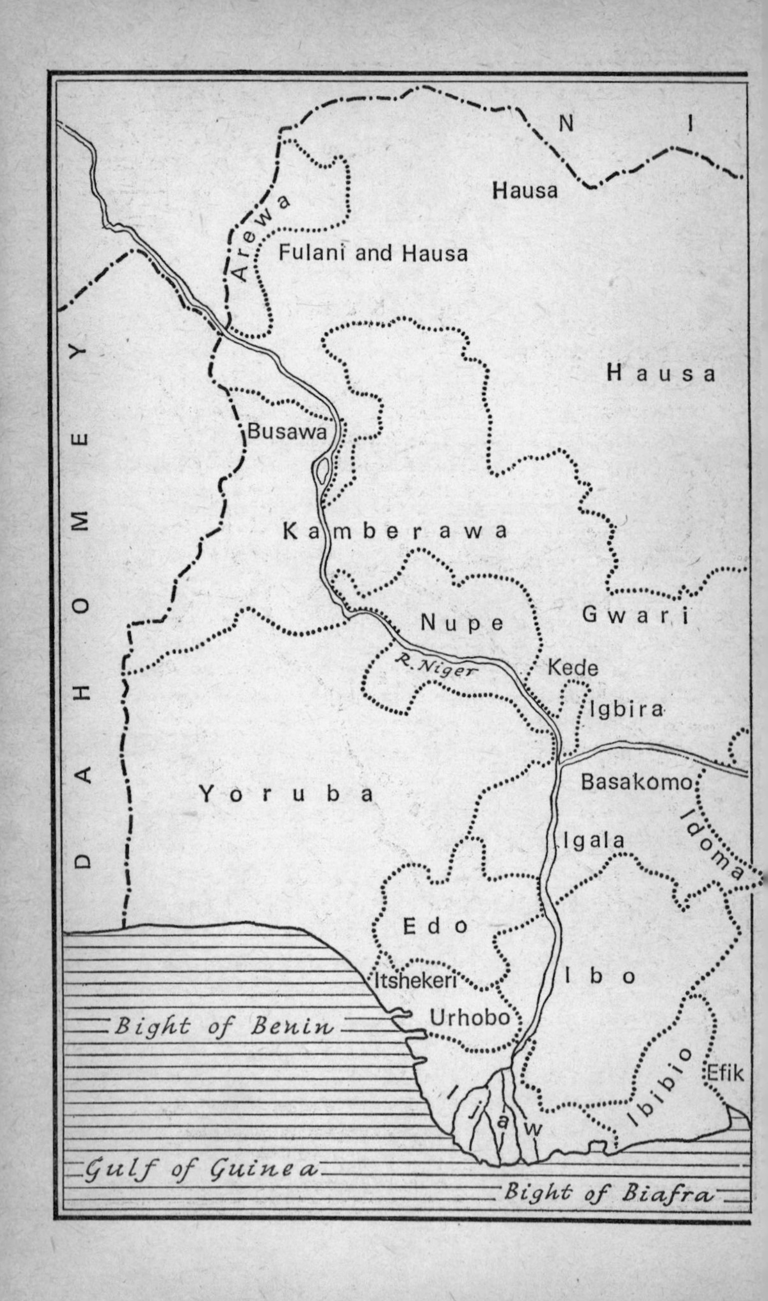
N I
Hausa
Arewa
Fulani and Hausa
DAHOMEY
Hausa
Busawa
Kamberawa
Nupe
Gwari
R. Niger
Kede
Igbira
Basakomo
Yoruba
Idoma
Igala
Edo
Itshekeri
Ibo
Urhobo
Bight of Benin
Efik
Ibibio
Ijaw
Gulf of Guinea
Bight of Biafra

G E R
TCHAD
Lake Chad
Buduma
Kanuri
and Fulani
Arab and Kanuri
Margi
Birom
R. Bewue
Bachama
Jukun
Tiv
Mambila
Iyalla
Ekoi
CAMEROUN REPUBLIC
Miles
0
150
0
Kilometres
240
Copyright © Federal Surveys, Nigeria, 1966

Additional Preface

Events in Nigeria have, since 29 July 1966, taken a new turn for the worse. The basic Nigerian objective – unity in diversity – has been put to its most severe test in living memory. And the irony is that the violence was sparked off by one of Major-General Aguiyi-Ironsi's boldest measures to promote the unity of the country. On 24 May, the National Military Government, encouraged by the prevailing popular mood for centralism, promulgated a decree (Decree no. 34 of 1966) which abolished the Regions of Nigeria and their federal form of government, unified the top grades of all the five public services and introduced a provincial system of administration. Five days later violent demonstration broke out in parts of Northern Nigeria, ostensibly in protest against the unification decree, resulting in destruction to the property and lives of many people of Eastern Nigerian origin. And these outbursts were a prelude to the holocaust which later swept across the country.

On 29 July, in the course of a reconciliation tour of the country, General Ironsi was kidnapped at Ibadan by some Northern Nigerian soldiers, and along with him his host, the Military Governor of Western Nigeria, Lieutenant-Colonel Fajuyi. This incident was followed by a week-end of bloodshed within the Army in which several Eastern Nigerian officers and other ranks were killed. After three days of widespread fear and doubt, Lieutenant-Colonel Yakubu Gowon emerged as General Aguiyi-Ironsi's successor.

In his first broadcast Lieutenant-Colonel Gowon announced that he would continue with the policies of his predecessor; but warned that the events of the previous seven months had convinced him that 'the basis for trust and confidence in our unitary system of government has not been able to stand the test of time.'

The 'base of unity' did not exist or had been so badly shaken that it was necessary for the people of Nigeria to review their political association in order 'to stop the country from drifting away into utter destruction'. He thought that a return to the constitutional position which existed before the introduction of the 'Unification Decree' was a necessary condition for resolving most of the problems which had brought disunity to the country. Accordingly, one of his first executive acts was the repeal of Decree no. 34 of 1966, and the return of the country to the federal form of government. All political prisoners were released, and within six weeks of assuming office Lieutenant-Colonel Gowon convened a Conference of Representatives of the Regional Governments to consider the form of political association suitable for Nigeria.

But in spite of these vigorous efforts to restore peace, tension mounted as the violence which started on 29 July continued to spread; and even while the Constitutional Conference then assembled in Lagos was drafting its interim report, murder and attacks on property increased in the North. These acts were severely condemned by the Supreme Commander and the Military Governor of the North, Lieutenant-Colonel Hassan Usman Katsina, and by all responsible Nigerians. Appropriate disciplinary action was taken by the authorities against those soldiers who participated in the terrible massacre of civilians at Kano on 30 September; but this incident, whatever the occasion for it, will remain a terrible blot in Nigerian history. Admittedly, Northerners and Easterners alike were victims of this wanton destruction; but the East has suffered incomparably more, and in addition to the sorrow and misery inflicted upon thousands of Eastern Nigerian households, there has been a full-scale exodus of Easterners from the North back to their homes, creating an unprecedented refugee problem for the Government of Eastern Nigeria.

Many reasons have been given for this tragic course of events: hatred and fear of the Ibo; the hunger for vengeance; the agitation of discredited politicians. Each of these factors may have contributed to the pogrom; but the pattern of destruction has revealed an essential nihilism rather than ideological or religious fervour. A few hours after news about the January coup broke in

Kaduna, gangs of young hoodlums attacked and looted the houses of Ministers as now discredited politicians. Five months later they destroyed life and property on a massive scale, ostensibly in protest against the alleged wrongs suffered by those same discredited politicians. Last September, men whose homes were situated more than thirty miles from the nearest post office or electricity supply looted telephone receivers, water heaters and refrigerators – household goods for which they did not have any use. The blind fury with which the mobs attacked anyone who stood in their way (many Northerners were killed by their own people) suggests that there are no short answers to why the riots happened or how to keep them from happening again. Meanwhile, Nigerian leaders are looking for political solutions. Many people believe that the right answers may be found in further loosening the constitutional ties which now hold the four Regions together. There are powerful advocates for a confederal system which will enable each Region to organize and control its separate army, police and currency – four sovereign states linked together by a common services organization. This arrangement, they believe, will eliminate all the areas of friction between the Regions. But, as the East African experience has shown, a common services organization is as likely to increase inter-unit friction as to promote peaceful cooperation. A confederation for so culturally heterogeneous a country as Nigeria will almost certainly end in a complete break-up and yet greater hostility between the different sovereign political units which will emerge. Independent armies facing each other across the border of sovereign Northern and Eastern Nigerias cannot be easily restrained from frequent clashes. The scars of history are hard to erase. Most leading Easterners give small support now to the objective of a united Nigeria; but, however difficult it may seem, this objective ought to be promoted as forcefully as possible. Regional (or tribal) chauvinism is incompatible with the development of a rising educated population and an expanding modern economy.

The most difficult solution – that of creating a nation out of the multiplicity of cultural groups – still seems to be the most effective. This implies the existence of a general government vested with independent taxing powers, able to control the import and export policy of the whole country and to command the loyalty of all its citizens. These ends can be achieved in spite of the powerful ethnic and cultural differences which divide the present generation of Nigerians. It is possible for us to have a high degree of economic integration and yet not interfere with one another's rate of social advancement. A common currency will not necessarily promote a strong federal union, but its economic advantages are overwhelming. As for the most serious source of friction – the control of the centre – we ought to experiment with a cooperative federal arrangement whereby all groups in the country will be represented in both the federal legislature and executive. To achieve these goals, the rest of the country must take all practical steps to heal the injuries inflicted upon the East, and the leaders of all groups must strive to lift the people out of the present conflicts and rally them behind the objective of unity in diversity.

Okoi Arikpo

Lagos
November 1966

Preface

The purpose of this book is not so much to record constitutional development in Nigeria as to try to explain how Nigeria came to be what it is today. Emphasis has, therefore, been laid on the social forces – political, economic and cultural – which have determined the nature and direction of constitutional change.

The central theme of the book is that Nigeria is neither a geographical expression nor a historical accident because, in spite of the bewildering variety of languages and customs found in the country, the people themselves are the progeny of two racial strains, negroid and hamitic, between which there has been continuous miscegenation for more than a thousand years, and because the physical features of the country – drainage system and vegetation zones – make it a single natural economic unit. Therefore, if British imperialism had not brought the inhabitants of the territory under one general government, some other social processes would have accomplished the same end. The only excuse I can offer for writing this book is that for ten years, between 1950 and 1960, I took some part, secondary though it was, in the process of trying to fashion a system by which Nigerians might live together as a free people; and I believe that part of the failures and difficulties which we now admit stem from the outright rejection by the one time powerful Nigerian political leaders of the political eclecticism which I, along with many Nigerians, advocated during those ten years.

The greater part of the manuscript was completed before the military coup of 15 January 1966. However, events since the coup tend to confirm rather than disprove my conclusion that, despite the difficulties of working a parliamentary system, Nigeria will continue as one country.

Non-Nigerian readers, unfamiliar with our propensity for

abbreviations, may find it helpful to know that the letters N.C.N.C. stand for the National Convention of Nigerian Citizens; N.P.C., for the Northern People's Congress; A.G., for Action Group; and N.N.D.P., for the Nigerian National Democratic Party. These were the political parties which at the time of the fall of the First Republic held sway in Nigeria. The N.N.D.P. and the N.P.C. together formed the Nigerian National Alliance (N.N.A.). The N.C.N.C. and A.G. together formed the United Progressive Grand Alliance (U.P.G.A.).

Finally (without the slightest intention of insulting the intelligence of any reader) I wish to state that this book is concerned with the 55 million people who live within the 356,000 square miles of territory on the Atlantic coast of West Africa between the Bight of Benin and the Bight of Biafra which is christened after the Niger, its principal river, **Nigeria.**

Okoi Arikpo

Lagos
March 1966

I. The People

Their physical environment, ethnic composition and cultural history

The most striking physical feature of Nigeria is the drainage system provided by its principal river, the Niger, and its tributary, the Benue. These two rivers, flowing from north-west and north-east down the middle of the territory into the sea, divide Nigeria into three land blocs, and provide relatively easy access into the heart of the country. And this feature has been of great significance in the history of Nigeria, because it was along the valleys of these two rivers that most ancestors of Nigeria's present inhabitants entered the country in ancient times. Other geographical factors which have influenced Nigeria's ethnic composition and cultural history are climate, vegetation and topography. The coastal belt which extends for nearly two hundred miles inland from the South Atlantic comprises a zone of high forest and heavy tropical rainfall. North of Ibadan from latitude 7°N the tropical rain forest gradually gives way to deciduous forest, which itself thins down into parkland from about latitude 10°N. Then right across the northern portion of the country from east to west between Sokoto and Maiduguri is a wide expanse of open terrain, which allowed a free movement of people and facilitated the intermingling of different races and cultures.

On the basis of distinct physical characteristics, two races may be distinguished in Nigeria – Negro and Hamite, neither of which now exists in its purest form. The distinctive physical characteristics of the Negro are a very dark, coffee-brown skin colour, thick heavy build, woolly hair and broad nose; and those of the Hamite, a light copper-bronze skin colour, tall stature, long slightly wavy hair and a narrow nose. These physical features in their purest forms exist only in a small proportion of the population today; but they occur in varying combinations in the overwhelming majority of the population in different parts of the country. The Ijaw of the Niger delta are perhaps the most Negroid of present-day Nigerians, and the cattle Fulani the purest of the Hamitic stock. Small enclaves of Arabs or Semites who have a common origin with the Hamites also exist in Kano, Sokoto, Zaria and in Bornu where they are known as the Shuwa Arabs.

Of the two races, the Negro was the first to arrive in Nigeria. His original home is still a matter of conjecture. Legends of origin ascribe to various places in Arabia and Asia Minor the source of various Negro groups; but the most plausible hypothesis, shaped from their many legends of origin and the very limited archaeological evidence yet available, suggests that north-east Africa was the area from which Negro tribes migrated westwards along the northern edge of the Congo basin, skirting the dense tropical forest and making use of the broad tract of parkland and semi-desert that extends across Africa south of the Sahara. Most of the Negro tribes entered what is now Nigeria across the Bornu plains, from where they fanned out in all directions; but the bulk of them moved along the valley of the Benue north-westwards to the Niger and north-east up the Gongola to the headwaters of Lake Chad. In this region, many of them settled from very early times as cultivators. Others spread south-westwards into the central Congo and later reached south-east Nigeria through the Cameroons, on their way absorbing sufficient Bantu cultural traits for their languages to take on a semi-Bantu character. Before the arrival of the Hamites, therefore, Negro tribes were spread all over the territory now called Nigeria.

Little is yet known about the early populations of Nigeria. The archaeological discoveries from the Nok valley in the Zaria province of Northern Nigeria indicate that at least by the first millennium B.C. there was a highly complex, settled, agricultural community in the area which in physique and culture was typically Negro. The Nok finds consist of terra-cotta figurines, statues, pottery, polished stone adzes, quartz beads and Acheulian axes. The figurines and statues portray highly stylized West African Negro physical features, an indication that the Nok people were the cultural ancestors of the present-day population of the central plains of Nigeria. The original Hausa (Habe) populations of Northern Nigeria, the Yoruba, the Nupe and their neighbours, appear from their epics and legends of origin to belong to the western stream of tribes, while the Ijaw, Ibibio, Ibo and Jukun must have been among those groups which migrated southwards along the valley of the Benue.

Hamites appear to have entered Nigeria from the Nile valley originally as Fulani nomadic herdsmen in search of grazing land. For many centuries, successive waves swept the open terrain of Northern Nigeria from Bornu to Sokoto; but then, some began to intermarry with the Hausa populations, which consisted in the main of sedentary Negro farmers, and to settle in villages. This penetration was at first peaceful and gradual, and by A.D. 1400 the Fulani seem to have settled across Hausaland in large numbers. At this time the Hausa in common with other Negro tribes were elaborating highly organized and complex nation-states, and so the original Negro population of Hausaland became physically modified through miscegenation with the immigrant Hamites long before the introduction of Islam in Northern Nigeria in the twelfth century or the rise of Fulani hegemony at the beginning of the nineteenth.

From the beginning of the first millennium A.D., several kingdoms or empires were established by Berber tribes, light-skinned people racially and culturally related to the Hamites, in the western Sudan to the north of present-day Nigeria. And some of these Sudanese kingdoms – Songhai, Kebbi, Kano, Kanem and Bornu perhaps most significantly[1] – have greatly influenced the cultural history and political structure of Nigeria.

In about A.D. 800 a group of Berber tribes from the Nile valley overran the Negro settlers of the Chad basin and established to the north and east of the Lake a non-Islamic kingdom called Kanem, whose rulers consolidated their position by assimilating the Negro tribes of the basin and gradually expanded the kingdom from the fringes of the Nile to the Niger and from the south of Fezzan to the mountains behind Dikwa. The Kanem empire included practically the whole of Hausaland, and by the eleventh century its rulers had accepted Islam. Then, in A.D. 1400, the Kanem empire disintegrated. The section to the east of Lake Chad broke up into small kingdoms, while the western sector, Kano, split off from Bornu. Bornu itself became the centre of the Kanuri nation, and the southern sector, comprising Bauchi and Gombe, was dominated by the Jukun to the south of Bornu.

At about the same period as one group of Berbers was establishing the kingdom of Kanem to the north-east of Nigeria, another group was founding the Songhai empire to the northwest. At the zenith of its power, Songhai extended from the Atlantic coast of West Africa to the borders of Bornu and northwards from the desert regions of Tripoli to Bussa on the Niger.

Kebbi and Kano were the most developed of the Hausa states, with Kano established about the same time as Bornu, and Kebbi some two hundred years later. Both states came alternately under Bornu and Songhai influence, and both have an interesting legend of origin in which the hero, Bawo, killed the sacred serpent that guarded the well at Daura and prevented people from drawing water there. The queen of Daura was so pleased at the death of the snake that she gave her daughter in marriage to Bawo, and out of that union were born the seven children who founded the seven Hausa states. Some versions of this legend say that Bawo was the son of Bayajidda, a grandson of the king of Baghdad, and that in addition to the seven legitimate sons there were seven illegitimate ones, who founded the kingdoms of Kebbi, Zamfara, Nupe, Gwari, Yoruba, Kwararafa (Jukun) – clearly an attempt to explain the generic connexion between the Hausa and their southern neighbours.

The Yoruba have a similar legend which ascribes their ancestral home to Mecca, whence their mythical ancestor, Oduduwa, was expelled by his Moslem neighbours for worshipping idols. Oduduwa and his followers fled westwards and finally reached Ife, where they settled. Oduduwa's eldest son had seven children, who founded the original seven kingdoms of the Yoruba. The seventh son, Oranyan, founded the Oyo kingdom; and after he had grown wealthy and powerful he decided to avenge his grandfather's humiliation. He set out with a large force of armed men towards Mecca but was intercepted by the Nupe on the Niger. He and his men fled to Bussa. The Chief of Bussa advised Oranyan to found a new city and, procuring a sacred snake as guide, advised Oranyan to follow the snake until it stopped in one place for seven days. If it then disappeared Oranyan should found his city at that place. Oranyan marched at the head of his forces behind the sacred snake, which travelled south and halted for seven days at a place called Ajaka, and then disappeared into the ground. Oranyan built his new city at that place and called it Oyo Ajaka, which is now known as Old Oyo.[2] Apart from any other inference that may be drawn from these legends of origin, it is reasonable to suppose that both the Hausa and the Yoruba arrived in Nigeria about the same time from the same area of north-east Africa and that they had cultural connexions dating back several centuries.

The basic social and political organization of the original Negro populations of Bornu and Hausaland was drastically modified by Berber invasions from the tenth to the thirteenth centuries, while the widespread conversion to Islam of the rulers in the western Sudan that began around A.D. 1000, and the establishment of commercial and cultural links across the Sahara with the Mediterranean world, substantially transformed the social and political systems of those inhabiting the savannah zone of Nigeria. But long before Islam became the official religion of the ruling classes, there had developed in Northern Nigeria complex political structures in which large populations spread over wide areas of territory were involved, and specialized crafts in metals, textiles and building had developed. From the similarities of these political systems and material cultures to those of the ancient civilizations of the Mediterranean and the Levant some ethnographers have drawn the inference that the earliest conquerors who subdued the small communities of cultivators came from the Levant.[3] In any event, by about A.D. 1000 the Hausa states were occupied by Berber races who came from the east and north across the desert and ruled at different periods as tributaries to Songhai and Bornu until displaced by the Fulani in 1807. The influence of these rulers extended south to the fringes of the coastal belt. It affected the political systems of the Nupe and Yoruba to the south and south-west, and of the Jukun to the south-east. The cultural interrelationships between the Yoruba and Bini are very well known. The Oba of Benin is by tradition regarded as a direct descendant of Oduduwa, founder of Ife, and the Benin political structure with its elaborate system of belief, in which the authority of king and chief is derived from their supernatural powers, is clearly of Yoruba origin. The famous Benin art of bronze-casting by the lost-wax process was introduced from Ife about the fifteenth century, and it played an important role in the development of kingship in Benin. Benin in turn influenced the Itshekeri, Urhobo Onitsha and Western Ibo, all of whom claim descent from Benin.

A branch of the Berbers who entered Bornu (the Zaghawa) moved southwards to the Benue area and founded the Jukun kingdom with its capital near Wukari. By A.D. 1500 they had occupied the whole of south-western Bornu and conquered most of the region of the Niger-Benue confluence, extending their influence east to the central Cameroons and south to the Bight of Biafra. They played a prominent part in the slave trade and were responsible for the widespread use of 'manillas' or copper-bar currency in the Benue region. The institutions of divine kingship and sun-worship, two Jukun cultural features, which have parallels in ancient Egyptian civilization, occur in many areas from the Igalla of the Niger-Benue confluence to the Ekoi in the south-eastern valley of the Cross river in south-eastern Nigeria.[4]

Although the autochthonous populations of Nigeria were, as has been shown, racially the same, centuries of separation into different areas of rule and the considerable new cultural influences introduced by immigrants from North Africa and the Middle East had by A.D. 1400 produced great differences between the peoples of the forest and savannah zones. While the latter were developing highly centralized, pyramidal political structures, and economic systems featuring occupational specialization and advanced agriculture, the former continued to be organized in small self-subsistent communities of cultivators and hunters, with a political organization still segmentary and kin-bound. Their art forms too, differed. The forest people (except for the Yoruba and Benin, whose art had been considerably influenced by Mediterranean culture) worked mainly in wood and iron and developed a hoe-culture, while the savannah people worked in brass and also developed a horse-culture. These cultural differences were accentuated by two events: European penetration from the coast and the rise of the Fulani at the beginning of the nineteenth century.

For centuries, the pastoral Fulani had wandered across the grasslands of Northern Nigeria with their herds, shifting with the seasons and seeking new pasture for their cattle. Many of them remained aloof from the local tribes of the country, but some settled in villages within the Hausa chiefdoms, intermarrying with the Hausa and attaining positions of influence and trust within the Hausa political hierarchy. In the eighteenth century they embraced Islam with fanaticism, and at the beginning of the nineteenth, they had become sufficiently influential to demand political power. Although Islam had been the official religion in most of the states of the western Sudan since the beginning of the twelfth century, there was very little evidence of religious fervour amongst the rulers of the Hausa states, and in a number of these states Moslems were persecuted. This aroused strong resentment among both Fulani and Hausa Moslems, and eventually the Fulani openly challenged the Hausa temporal power. The revolt was led by Othman Dan Fodio, the son of the head of the Torankawa Fulani, who migrated into Gobir from the kingdom of Melle after its destruction by the Songhai kingdom. A devout Moslem and a most influential religious teacher, Dan Fodio rallied to the cause of Islam Fulani and Hausa alike. In 1804, open warfare broke out between the Fulani under his leadership and the Chief of Gobir. The war soon spread to other Hausa states, and although initially there was a strong religious element in the Fulani rising, it gradually became a war of conquest, and one Hausa state after another was conquered by Dan Fodio and his Fulani flag-bearers. By 1808 the Fulani were in control of all Hausaland, and a new empire had been established under Fulani hegemony.

The empire had its centre at Sokoto, and extended from Marata (outside the present northern boundary of Nigeria) down to Ilorin, and from the middle Niger across to the western boundaries of Bornu, encompassing the present emirates of Katsina, Kano, Zaria, Hadejia, Daura, Adamawa, Bauchi, Katagum, Gombe, Nupe and Ilorin. Politically, it was organized through a number of theocratic principalities or emirates, ruled over by Emirs who owed allegiance to the Sultan of Sokoto as the Sarkin Musulimi or Commander of the Faithful. These Emirs paid annual tribute, usually in slaves, to the Sultan to whom they owed their thrones and who from time to time interfered in their internal affairs. The administration of the emirates themselves was highly centralized and pyramidal. At the apex was the Emir whose personality commanded religious reverence, and his order absolute obedience. Then, under him, there was a hierarchy of officials who administered a code of law, through judicial tribunals, and a regular system of taxation. The emirate organization had all the authoritarian features of the medieval Islamic state, and as the driving force of this system was the Fulani aristocracy of Sokoto, who lived on the tributes and gifts from the empire, in slaves and farm produce, the Emirs themselves were obliged constantly to raid neighbouring tribes for slaves, so that vast areas of territory on the central plain of Nigeria were depopulated by them.

But the Fulani empire was at no time co-terminous with the area now called Northern Nigeria. To the north-east, the Kanuri of Bornu, under the leadership of Muhammed El Kanemi, successfully stemmed the tide of Fulani expansion. Further south, along the Benue valley, the Jukun were repeatedly raided for slaves and driven to the southern bank of the river, but they were never brought within the ambit of the Fulani empire, largely owing to their rejection of Islam, their doctrine of divine kingship, and their devotion to their cults and their King, whom they believed to be a supernatural being and the guarantor of fertility. The tribes on the rugged central Jos plateau, too, were free from Fulani domination, protected by their surroundings from control by the Hausa kingdoms. South of Ilorin, the Yoruba constantly fought to keep out Fulani assailants, and the Tuaregs to the north never gave up their fight for independence from Sokoto. Consequently, the Fulani empire experienced internal rebellions and civil wars, along with a decline in the Islamic fervour, widespread graft and corruption, and a breakdown in the military organization upon which stability rested. The final overthrow of the Fulani overlords by the British in 1903 prevented, indeed, the collapse and disintegration of the Fulani political system, which was to constitute the administrative framework of Northern Nigeria under colonial rule and the independent government of the First Republic. And before their overthrow, the Fulani had, within a century, succeeded in bringing under a unified political system nearly three-quarters of the territory which is now Nigeria. They had spread Islam to nearly two-thirds of the inhabitants of the country and along with it the culture of the Mediterranean and the Levant.

At about the same period that the Hausa states were elaborating their complex political organization, the Yoruba to the south-west of the Niger were establishing new kingdoms under leaders who claimed descent from the legendary Oduduwa.[5] East of the Niger political organization appears to have remained segmentary, and no elaborate state organization came into being anywhere in the Eastern Provinces before A.D. 1500. Around this latter period, however, a number of city-states developed, mainly along the coast and the principal trade routes. Thus, by the beginning of the sixteenth century, when European penetration of Nigeria began to make its impact, the originally homogeneous populations of the territory were already developing along different lines, physically and culturally. And this separate development continued until the tiny island of Lagos, once a Benin military outpost and later the most important slave-mart on the West African coast, became the first step in the establishment of a British colony.

It is usual to speak today of the three large Nigerian Regions as corresponding to the ethnic divisions of the country. The North is said to be inhabited by Hausa-Fulani; the West, by Yoruba; and the East, by Ibo. But this description is very far from the actual facts. In the North, for instance, there are, in addition to the Hausa and Fulani, at least one hundred other linguistic groups, large and small. Some of them are well known even beyond the boundaries of Nigeria. The Tiv, who number one million, are widely celebrated for their resistance to Fulani hegemony. The Birom, Nupe, Idoma, Igalla and Igbirra are among some of the larger linguistic groups distinguishable. The estimated population of Northern Nigeria in mid-1953 was some 17,153,712 in all, of whom 8·5 millions were Hausa-Fulani; 1·2 million, Kanuri; 400,000, Nupe; and some 7 million, others. The Hausa, Fulani, Kanuri and Nupe have long embraced Islam, adopted Hausa as a *lingua franca*, and accepted the system of administration based on the Emir and a feudal pyramid of officials and functionaries below him. They can, therefore, be regarded as a culturally homogeneous group. The remaining 7 million of the population belong to the vast number of other linguistic and cultural groups, and though a third of them are adherents of Islam, the rest are either animists or Christians.

In the West (before the creation of the Mid-West Region), several significant linguistic groups were identifiable in addition to the dominant Yoruba group. Out of an estimated mid-1953 population of 6·2 million, there were about one million Edo-speaking (Bini) people, half a million Urhobo, 365,000 Western Ibo, and over 80,000 Ijaw. Similarly, in the East the estimated mid-1953 population of 7·3 million included about 1·5 million Efik-Ibibio speaking peoples, half a million Ekoi-Yakurr speakers, and another half a million Ijaw- and Ogoni-speaking peoples.[6] No Region of Nigeria is, therefore, culturally homogeneous. On the other hand, a study of the folklore, traditions of origin, and language-structure of many of the tribes reveals cultural inter-connexions which cut across Regional and administrative boundaries. We have already spoken of the cultural inter-relationships between the Yorubas and Edo (Bini), with the Oba of Benin by tradition regarded as a direct descendant of Oduduwa, the founder of Ife, and of how the Itshekeri, Urhobo, Ika, Asaba and Onitsha people across the Niger and its delta all in turn claim descent from Benin and incorporate features of Benin kingship in their own traditional forms. Across the Northern border, the Igalla-speaking peoples of Kabba province claim a common origin with the Yoruba and Bini, and the Atah of Igalla, the traditional head chief, wears a brass mask which is most probably of early Benin workmanship. Igalla Chiefs, like their Benin counterparts, wear beads on their wrists as a symbol of their office; and in both Igalla and Benin the death of the King used to be kept secret for a period of one to three years. Furthermore, the Igalla language belongs to the same linguistic group as Edo and Yoruba; but Igalla is also closely related to the language of the Idoma further east, and Idoma is in turn related to Iyala, a language widely spoken in parts of the Ogoja province of Eastern Nigeria. According to Armstrong,[7] these linguistic relationships may be explained by the hypothesis that the various groups derive from a single social group, parts of which have at various times become separated, and have developed different forms of kingship and political institutions. To fit the whole pattern of the different linguistic and cultural groups of Nigeria together would be the work of a life-time; but the completed puzzle would reveal that, diverse as the people of Nigeria appear to be, they cannot be divided into well-defined areas of distinct physique, language-group and material culture. They are drawn from the same 'box of bricks' though the bricks are arranged in different patterns. Many of the differences have arisen from the territorial distribution of the peoples, variations in the social environment, and the external cultural influences to which the peoples have been subjected.

2. European Penetration

Exploration, trade, occupation and administrative control

At about the same time as the Fulani were entering the Hausa states of Kano, Gobir and Katsina in large numbers, the first European explorers and traders appeared on the coast of Nigeria. In 1472, Portuguese explorers, sailing south-east along the Gulf of Guinea, discovered the coastline of Nigeria, and Ruy de Seguina, commanding one of the expeditions, landed on the island of Lagos, at that time a military outpost of the kingdom of Benin. He succeeded in making contact with the Oba (King) of Benin but did not on this occasion reach Benin City. In 1485 another Portuguese trader, Alfonsa d'Aveiro, reached Benin and was well received by the Oba. He returned to Portugal with a cargo of red pepper, hitherto obtainable only from India and the Far East; and before long the Portuguese developed a lucrative trade with Benin in pepper, ivory, gold and slaves. For sixty years, indeed, the Portuguese successfully maintained a monopoly in the trade of the Guinea Coast, as the area of the Bight of Benin came to be known, establishing diplomatic relations with Benin, and exchanging 'ambassadors'.

King John II of Portugal sent many factors and officers to the court of the Oba and set up trading stations at many points along the Benin river. But at last, in 1553, the Portuguese trade monopoly was broken by the English. In that year a Captain Windham and his party of sailors reached Benin and procured eighty tons of pepper. The English were quickly followed by the French, Dutch and Danes, and for the next three hundred years a large volume of trade, mainly in slaves, developed along the coast of Nigeria.

In this trade Britain took a leading part, and by the Treaty of Utrecht in 1712 secured a thirty-year monopoly in the 'carrying trade', a monopoly which greatly enchanced British prestige along the west coast.[8] In exchange for the slaves and other commodities which they exported, the African middlemen received goods which included metals, silks, damasks, jewellery, spirits, muskets and gunpowder. The trade in firearms was especially esteemed, because its control was a source of economic and political power. Its acquisition by the middlemen facilitated their establishment of strong city states along the coast – Lagos, Brass, Bonny Calabar – in the sixteenth and seventeenth centuries. For four hundred years, the European traders confined their activities to the coast and a few miles inland along the estuaries of the principal rivers. The coastal Chiefs opposed their penetration of the hinterland and denied them the right to occupy any territory. Certainly, long before the arrival of the Europeans, slave-raiding had gone on in the grassland areas of the interior of Nigeria, with large numbers of slaves exported across the desert to the Mediterranean and the Near East. Arabs, Fulanis and Negroes had engaged in slave-raiding, but the inaccessibility of the rain forest region to cavalry had left the people of this area in comparative safety. With the introduction of European firearms, however, that comparative safety disappeared over a wide area of the rain forest region, and many of the slaves loaded at the coast into European ships had already travelled many hundreds of miles through the valleys of the Benue and the Niger.

Roman Catholic priests from Portugal pressed hard on the heels of the explorers and traders, and in 1486 the first missionaries arrived in Benin to act as 'holy advisers to the King of Benin, to convert him to the faith of our Lord Jesus Christ, commanding him earnestly to forsake his idolatories and fetishes which the negroes used and practised in his lands'.

By 1514 the King's son and many of his subjects, though not the King himself, had become Christians. Church buildings were erected not only in Benin but in many of the Portuguese trading posts along the Niger delta, between Brass and Warri; but despite two hundred years of Catholic effort, Christianity flickered out and was not revived until the arrival of Protestant missionaries during the first half of the nineteenth century. This was a period of great evangelical revival and of strong public revulsion against the slave trade. It was also an era of exploration and intense commercial interest in Africa. The missionaries were in part anxious to purge the guilt of their country for the slave trade by saving the souls of those whose lives and homes had been shattered. The industrialists were equally anxious to win the vast potential markets of West Africa for their products. In 1841 a liberated Negro slave, the Reverend Ajayi Crowther, accompanied the Niger Expedition to explore the possibilities of evangelical work among the inhabitants of the delta. In the following year another clergyman of Negro descent, the Reverend Thomas Birch Freeman, a Wesleyan minister, landed at Badagry and began to preach there; further to the east a Church of Scotland party under the Reverend Hope Masterton Waddell established an outpost at Calabar in 1846; and in 1855 the first organized body of missionaries sent to Nigeria by the Church of England landed at Badagry and established a mission station.[9] The missionaries, unlike the traders, were able to penetrate the hinterland. From Badagry, the Anglicans and Methodists spread the gospel as far inland as Ijebu-Ode, Abeokuta and Oyo; from Calabar the Scottish mission moved up the Cross river and established stations at many points along it.

Towards the end of the eighteenth century yet another motive, the scientific, drew Europeans into Nigeria. In 1788, an African Association was formed in London to promote the exploration of the continent's interior, and it dispatched several expeditions through north-west Africa. One of these expeditions, undertaken by Mungo Park, reached the Niger at Segu in July 1796, and another reached Bussa, where Mungo Park was driven back in 1805. Other expeditions were sent out between 1805 and 1830, when Richard Lander and his brother succeeded in tracing the course of the Niger from Bussa down to the multitude of creeks and rivers now known as the Niger delta.

This discovery was recognized as one of great scientific and commercial importance, and immediate attempts were made to open up trade with the interior of Nigeria through the Niger. Several expeditions were sent to explore the Niger delta, to survey the main stream as far north as it could be navigated, and to establish trading depots. There was considerable opposition from the local inhabitants, who had hitherto been middlemen between the people of the hinterland and European traders on the coast. Indeed, the efforts of the earlier explorers, Denham, Clapperton and Oudney, were impeded by some of the Chiefs and Arab traders who feared that the visit of these explorers was a prelude to keen commercial competition by Europeans and interference in the slave trade itself.

When in 1807 the slave trade was abolished in Britain by Act of Parliament, it was decided by the government of the day that in order to stamp out effectively the 'carrying trade', a British naval squadron should be stationed on the West African coast to prevent foreign ships from engaging in the trade. The squadron patrolled up and down the Gulf of Guinea from Cape Verde to Fernando Po, keeping an incessant watch for slavers on the beaches of Whydah, Badagry and Lagos and at the mouths of the Niger, Bonny and Cross rivers. A British naval expedition was even sent up the Niger, to sail as far as the confluence of the Niger and Benue rivers and sign treaties of friendship with the Chiefs of Abo and Ida, where land was obtained for the purpose of establishing a farm settlement for liberated slaves.

Within a short time, however, the expedition was obliged to withdraw to Fernando Po owing to the spread of malaria among many of the officers and men. Meanwhile, another British government-sponsored expedition set out from Tripoli in North Africa under a German physician, Dr Barth, and visited Katsina, Kano, and Kukawa (Bornu), concluding treaties of friendship and trade with the rulers of these emirates. A third naval expedition set out in 1854 and sailed up the Niger and its tributary, the Benue, as far inland as Muri; and in 1857 a fourth expedition went up the Niger as far as Jebba, where the steamer struck a rock and sank.

These expeditions, apart from providing geographical information, confirmed the great possibilities of trade with the interior of Nigeria by way of the river Niger and its tributaries; but the trade could only be carried out on the banks of the river under naval protection. Further inland the rulers and Chiefs would not brook the presence in their midst of strangers who would deprive them of their middlemen's profits and in any way interfere with their established traditions and pattern of social organization. The British answer to their challenge was the formation in 1886 of a government-sponsored quasi-military trading organization, the Royal Niger Chartered Company, which exercised a monopoly of the trade on the river, maintained an armed constabulary, exercised judicial authority, imposed taxes, and collected customs duties. The Company performed all the functions of an independent government, indeed, except that it had not the right to negotiate with foreign powers.

Along the coast the British naval blockade became progressively more effective with the development of legitimate trade in palm oil, and by 1840 there was very little export of slaves from Bonny and Calabar, although the slave market of Dahomey was still being fully fed by captives from the Yoruba wars. The palm oil trade was still conducted from hulks moored along the mouths of the rivers away from the beaches; and it was controlled by the coastal Chiefs, who imposed a customs duty, called 'Comey'. In return for this tax, the coastal Chiefs ensured that there was a regular supply of produce from the hinterland and that the market prices were well regulated. But despite this mechanism, the European traders had very little protection, either from their fellow traders or from obstreperous African middlemen, and had to depend on the British naval squadron based at Fernando Po. As the coastal Chiefs became wealthier and more powerful, the traders became more nervous and asked for better protection from the British Government. In answer to their repeated demands, the British Government then appointed Consuls, whose function was to protect and assist British subjects trading or residing on the West Coast, with the first of them, Beecroft, assigned the Bights of Benin and Biafra in 1849, from headquarters in Fernando Po.

In 1853, Campbell was appointed Consul for Lagos, and there began a struggle for the control of Lagos which culminated in the Treaty of Cession in 1861. Consuls had no executive authority over British subjects on the coast and were invested with no judicial powers over the subjects of the territories to which they were accredited, notwithstanding the provisions of the Foreign Jurisdiction Act of 1843, which conferred on the representatives of the Queen 'within divers territories and places out of Her Majesty's Dominions' the right to exercise and enjoy any Power or jurisdiction in 'as ample a manner as if Her Majesty had acquired such Powers or Jurisdiction by Cession or conquest of territory.' But the Consuls, backed by British gunboats, quickly rose to power by their bold intervention in the domestic politics of the coastal states. At first they used their power to support the exploitation of the coastal trade by the unscrupulous 'palm oil ruffians', the epithet applied to European traders of that period, and when African commercial rivalry had been successfully crushed, they turned to political control of these states. Gunboat diplomacy was so successful on the coast, indeed, especially with the small city-states, that 'when King Archibong of Calabar died in 1852, Beecroft presided over the election of the new king, and his right to do so was never questioned.'[10] Everywhere the Consuls supported and flattered those Nigerian rulers who espoused the British cause in trade, religion and political influence; and harassed and intrigued against those who challenged British supremacy. The classic example of the new diplomacy emerged in the struggle over the succession to the throne of Lagos.

By 1850 the strategic value of Lagos as a base from which to crush the slave-trading kingdom of Dahomey, as a commercial centre and key to the hinterland of Nigeria, had become clear. The reigning King of Lagos, Kosoko, was a strong ally of Dahomey and a supporter of the slave trade; so, to oust Kosoko from Lagos, Consul Beecroft approached Kosoko's docile uncle Akitoye, from whom Kosoko had wrested the throne, in his exile at Badagry. He offered to restore Akitoye to his throne if the latter would agree to sign a treaty for the abolition of the slave trade in the Bight of Benin and to promote legitimate trade with British merchants. Akitoye readily accepted the offer; in 1851 Lagos was attacked by a British naval squadron, and after four days of fierce fighting was captured.

Akitoye kept his side of the bargain, signing a treaty with Great Britain whereby he agreed to abolish the slave trade, to protect Christian missionaries and to promote legitimate trade. But the return of Akitoye to the Lagos throne brought no peace to the island and fighting went on intermittently between his supporters and those of his rival, Kosoko, who had been driven out of Lagos. By the time Akitoye died in 1854 he was a mere puppet of Campbell, who had succeeded Beecroft as Consul for the Bight of Benin in 1853. Akitoye's son Dosumu, who was installed by Campbell on Akitoye's death, was no less docile than his father, and on 6 August 1861 he was coerced by Campbell to cede the island of Lagos altogether. Under the Treaty of Cession, Dosumu transferred the port and island of Lagos, 'together with rights, profits, territories and appurtenances thereunto attached', absolutely to the British Crown, in consideration of the payment to him of an annual pension, the right to continue to use the title of 'King', and the right to decide disputes among the indigenes of Lagos, with their consent and subject to appeal to British laws.

Lagos became a British colony; Consul Campbell was appointed its Governor; and a Legislative Council was established to make laws for its administration. In 1862, the Settlement of Lagos, as it was then called, was placed under the jurisdiction of the Governor-in-Chief of the West African possessions, with headquarters at Freetown, Sierra Leone, and shortly afterwards the surrounding districts were annexed in quick succession. Palma and Lekki were ceded by Kosoko in 1863; and Badagry by the Akran and his Chiefs in the same year. Then Addo and Oke Odan were declared protectorates of Lagos. Attempts were made to post British Consuls in Ijebu Ode and Abeokuta; but the Yoruba, shocked by the annexation of Lagos, refused to trade with the government there. Indeed, between 1863 and 1875, many attempts were made by the Egbas to neutralize the spread of British influence in Yorubaland. In 1872, the Egbas blockaded the trade route between Lagos and the Yoruba hinterland; and as a reprisal, Glover, who was then the Administrator of Lagos, introduced a Bill in the Legislative Council on 20 March 1872, for 'an Ordinance to Empower the Administrator of the Settlement of Lagos in certain cases to shut the roads to the interior by proclamation', in the hope that blockading the roads against the Egbas and Ijebus would cause the rest of the Yoruba to rebel.

An open rupture between the Lagos Government and the Egbas, he believed, would be immediately followed by a rupture between those two Yoruba groups and the rest of Yorubaland. The merchants in Lagos thought differently and they addressed a petition to the Administrator pointing out that although the Egbas had closed the road against produce being sent to Lagos, the prohibition on the export of merchandise from Lagos to Abeokuta would ruin the Lagos merchants. When Glover forced the Bill through the four-member Legislative Council, the merchants sent a deputation of both Europeans and Africans to Pope-Hennessy, the Governor-in-Chief of the West African Possessions, to protest against the Bill. Glover then summoned a meeting of the Legislative Council on 6 May 1872, to secure support for his action, claiming in his address that the object of the deputation was to induce the British Government by guile to withdraw the Lagos Administration and surrender the Settlement. The European merchants might think that they were guiding and directing the 'Native Egba merchants' who accompanied the Europeans in the deputation, but in fact the 'Native Sierra Leone Egba merchants' were using the European merchants for their own purpose, which was the withdrawal of British rule from Lagos.

Alarmed by this report, the Legislative Council adopted a motion requesting the Governor-in-Chief to visit Lagos with 'a man-of-war, the Colonial Steamer, Eko, and the Hausa Force which had been withdrawn from Lagos'.[11] Glover's threats did not appear to have been very effective, for in 1873 the Legislative Council of Lagos was abolished and the colony was administered from Accra as the Eastern Provinces of the Gold Coast until 1886, when it was again established as a separate colony, with its own Legislative and Executive Councils under its own Governor and Commander-in-Chief.[12]

It was vital to the strategic and commercial value of Lagos that Yorubaland should come under the influence of the Lagos Government, and so in July 1886, the new Governor, Sir William Macgregor, persuaded the Alafin of Oyo, the Oni of Ife, the Owa of Ilesha, the Awujale of Ijebu and other Yoruba Chiefs, except the Alake of Abeokuta, where there was civil war, to sign a treaty of peace, friendship and commerce. By this treaty the Chiefs agreed to maintain and promote peace among themselves; to submit themselves to such directions as might seem necessary or expedient to the Governor of Lagos; to preserve the existing boundaries (except for some minor readjustments); and to refer all their disputes to arbitration by the Governor of Lagos, peaceably awaiting his determination of any dispute and abiding by his decision once it was given.

This treaty not only brought peace into Yorubaland; it halted the threat of French expansion into the region. The road was now open for the advance of Lagos into Western Nigeria, and the Lagos Government made maximum use of the opportunity. In 1891, a protectorate was declared over Ilaro and the Egbado district, and in 1892 Ijebu Ode was occupied by troops of the Lagos Government. The southern districts of Ijebuland were annexed to the colony of Lagos, and the Ijebus, thus outflanked to the south and west, accepted British protection and the control of their administration by a British Resident in 1894. Abeokuta was now isolated, and to ward off the threat of the British advance, the Alake and his Chiefs signed a treaty of friendship and commerce with the Governor of Lagos by which they agreed, in consideration of the Governor's promise not to annex any portion of Egba territory, to promote free trade between Lagos and Egbaland; not to close any road without the consent of the Governor; to protect and assist all ministers of the Christian religion; and to submit disputes between British citizens and Egba citizens to the Governor for settlement as he deemed expedient.

The treaty was followed by the demarcation of boundaries between Lagos and Egbaland and the establishment of the United Egba National Government. Meanwhile, Oyo had surrendered her independence and become a British Protectorate. The Alafin signed a treaty with the Governor of Lagos pledging himself to facilitate the free movement of British subjects throughout Yorubaland; to protect Christian missionaries; and never to enter into any treaty with any foreign government except through the British Government. Six months after the signing of the Oyo treaty all Yorubaland, except Egbaland, had become a British Protectorate, and Lagos now set out to weld into one political entity the different (and often warring) peoples who occupied the land mass between the Bights of Benin and Biafra and the southern fringes of the Sahara by the construction of a railway line from Lagos to Ibadan in 1894.

At the same time as Lagos and the Yoruba country were being drawn into the British sphere of influence, the British Consul for the Bight of Biafra was busy securing 'Treaties of Protection' from most of the coastal and riverain chiefs in Eastern Nigeria. In consequence of these treaties, Britain was able to claim at the historic Berlin West African Conference that all the coast and much of the hinterland of Nigeria fell within her sphere of influence; and immediately after that conference, the coastal area was declared a British Protectorate, named the Oil Rivers Protectorate, with headquarters at Calabar in Eastern Nigeria. Administered by a Commissioner and Consul-General directly responsible to the British Foreign Office, the area of the Protectorate was gradually enlarged, so that by 1893 it included the whole of the territory between Lagos and the Cameroons border in the south, extending northwards along the Niger up to Onitsha. It became known as the Niger Coast Protectorate.

To the north of this area was the territory administered by the Royal Niger Company under its charter, extending from Ilorin in the south-west to Bornu in the north-east, and from Sokoto in the north-west to Ibi on the Benue. Practically the whole of Nigeria was now under British control, but for fifteen years that control was exercised through three separate authorities: the Colonial Office, which administered Lagos and its districts; the Foreign Office, which exercised control over the Niger Coast Protectorate; and the Royal Niger Company, which controlled the riverain areas of the Niger and Benue valleys. This tripartite control was ended on the first day of January 1900: an Order-in-Council was promulgated whereby the Niger Coast Protectorate and the Royal Niger Company's territory south of Idah on the Niger were proclaimed the Protectorate of Southern Nigeria; the area to the north of Idah became the Protectorate of Northern Nigeria; and Lagos with the surrounding districts became the Colony and Protectorate of Lagos.

All three administrative units were placed under the general jurisdiction of the British Colonial Office; but each unit followed a separate course of development, with a separate government, a separate staff, and its own quite distinct theory and system of administration. The Protectorate of Northern Nigeria initially comprised a long narrow corridor of territory on both banks of the Niger from Idah to Yauri and along the valley of the Benue up to Ibi. The rest of Northern Nigeria was either controlled by the Fulani under Sokoto hegemony or was organized in small pagan village communities still fighting against Fulani domination; slave-raiding by Fulani and Arab adventurers was still a common feature of life in the plains of the region. The first task of the High Commissioner, Sir Frederick (later Lord) Lugard, on his assumption of office, was to establish the 'pax Britannica' over the whole territory, including areas not covered by 'Friendship Treaties'. The early years of Lugard's administration were, therefore, largely devoted to punitive expeditions against recalcitrant Fulani Emirs and pagan tribes. One by one the Emirs were subjugated, from

Bida to Bornu and from Kano to Sokoto, and as each Emir was defeated he was deposed and replaced by another person more amenable to the new government. Each new Emir at his installation was given a letter of appointment setting out the conditions under which he held his command: that he recognized the Protectorate Government as the supreme authority over his emirate; that he would rule justly; would forbid slave-raiding in his area of jurisdiction; and that the land within his emirate, together with all minerals therein, was vested in the Crown in trust for the people of the emirate. This accepted, the Emirs were allowed to carry on in much the same way as they had done before, except that the most corrosive features of Fulani rule were prohibited.[13] From this administrative expedient of governing through the Fulani Emirs grew the theory and practice of indirect rule, which later became one of the most distinctive features of British colonial policy in Africa.

By contrast, the administration of the Southern Protectorate was from the beginning direct. Each officer of the administration was the principal executive and magisterial authority of the district under his charge, and he administered its people and their affairs directly. Secondly, because there was very little resistance to British domination by the end of the nineteenth century, the administration of the Southern Protectorate was able from the start to devote its energies to the construction of roads and a railway and to the development of trade. Finally, whereas in the North the Protectorate Government undertook not to interfere with the spread of Islam, thereby restricting the activities of Christian missionaries, in the South Christian missionaries were encouraged to expand both their religious and educational activities. The resultant effect of these widely differing policies was a further widening in the outlook between the people of the North and South.

The Colony of Lagos had from its establishment (except for a brief period between 1873 and 1885) had a Legislative Council. In 1906, by Letters Patent and Royal Instructions, the administrations of Lagos and the Protectorate of Southern Nigeria were merged into the Colony and Protectorate of Southern Nigeria, and the Legislative Council of the Colony was empowered to legislate for the Southern Nigeria Protectorate in all matters in which the British Crown had acquired jurisdiction.

3. Constitutional Evolution (1914–47)

From Crown Colony to Protectorate

In November 1913 the Nigeria Protectorate Order-in-Council was issued to bring under one general government the territories hitherto known as the Colony and Protectorate of Southern Nigeria and the Protectorate of Northern Nigeria, and on New Year's Day 1914 the new political entity known as the Colony and Protectorate of Nigeria – **NIGERIA** for short – appeared on the world map, in the red shading of the British Empire. Sir Frederick Lugard became its first Governor-General, with Lagos its capital and principal seat of government. Directly under the Governor-General were a Lieutenant-Governor for the Northern Provinces (based at Zungeru), another Lieutenant-Governor for the Southern Provinces (based in Lagos), and an Administrator of the Colony.

The Order-in-Council made provision for the establishment of an enlarged Executive Council and an advisory and deliberative body known as the Nigerian Council whose functions would be exercised in respect of the whole of Nigeria, although Lagos still retained its Legislative Council. This Nigerian Council was set up early in 1914 with a membership of 42, including all the members of the Executive Council (23 officials), 7 European and 6 Nigerian unofficial members representing business interests, and 6 other Nigerian unofficial members nominated by the Governor-General. The Council had neither executive nor legislative authority. Indeed, the Order-in-Council which created it expressly provided that:

> No resolution passed by the Council shall have any legislative or executive authority, and the Governor shall not be required to give effect to any such resolution unless he thinks fit and is authorized to do so.

The title of Governor-General was personal to Lugard. His successors in office were designated Governor.

The 6 other Nigerian representatives were 2 Emirs from the North, the Alafin of Oyo, 1 member from Lagos, 1 from Calabar, and 1 from the Warri-Benin area. The 3 Chiefs were supposed to represent the views of the masses of the people. However, they very seldom attended meetings of the Council, even though these were few and far between, and on the rare occasions when their robes adorned the Chamber, they took no part in the deliberations. Between 1914 and December 1920 the Council held a total of seven meetings. Indeed, so ineffective was the Nigerian Council that Sir Hugh Clifford in 1924 described it as 'a debating society in which nobody would enter into a debate', and its meetings as 'those dreary, apathetic, feeble, faint, colourless, meaningless meetings that used to weary us all so intensely in the past'. The First World War (1914–18) brought the work of amalgamation and development to an abrupt halt. Attention was diverted from constitutional and political issues. Nigerian soldiers were fighting the Germans in the Cameroons and in East Africa. Educated Nigerians demonstrated their loyalty to the British Crown by shelving all demands for constitutional change. The First World War was 'a war to end all wars and make democracy safe'. The people of Nigeria demonstrated their faith in the British Empire by maintaining a degree of calm and peace which had not been known in the country before.

Soon after the end of the war, however, the clamour for constitutional change began in earnest, particularly in Lagos. African professionals, backed by the local newspapers, demanded a representative legislature and were supported in this by some European residents. For instance, at the meeting of the Nigerian Council held at Lagos in December 1919, a European unofficial member named Robert McNeill, representing commercial interests, set down the following motion for debate:

> That this Council be either reconstructed so as to make it a serious factor in governing this Colony and Protectorate or be abolished.

The motion was not pressed to a division because the Governor, realizing the unanimity of opinion among African and European (including even official) members, intervened in the debate to announce that he would undertake a serious study of the matter and make representations to the Secretary of State for the Colonies on reforms to make the Council

> a serious factor in the government of the Colony and Protectorate and also as truly and practically representative of all Nigerian interests as was possible for any Assembly of the kind, having regard to the vastness of the country and the great diversity of race, culture, political and social institutions, of language and religious beliefs which obtain among its inhabitants.[14]

The demand for a representative legislature was echoed at the first meeting of the National Congress of British West Africa which was held in Accra in 1920.* The resolutions of the Accra Conference drew a long and bitter attack from the Governor, Sir Hugh Clifford, who declared in his address to the Nigerian Council at its meeting on 29 December 1920:

> There has during the last few months been a great deal of loose and gaseous talk on the subject of popular election of Members of Council in Nigeria – talk which has for the most part emanated from a self-selected and a self-appointed congregation of educated African gentlemen who collectively style themselves the West African National Congress. Europe and West Africa are, alike, geographical expressions. The peoples of West Africa do not belong to the same stock and are not of common descent. They are bound together by no common language. They have no community of religious belief. The nations of Europe have this, at least, in common that they have evolved for themselves analogous social and political systems, which though they differ from one another in detail, are all based upon the same general principles.

He described as 'farcical' the suggestion that

> continental Nigeria can be represented by a handful of gentlemen drawn from a half dozen coast tribes – men born and bred in British-administered towns situated on the sea-shore, who in the safety of British protection, have peacefully pursued their studies under British teachers in British schools in order to enable them to become ministers of religion or learned in the laws of England. These self-appointed spokesmen of sixteen million Nigerians have never penetrated into the interior at all.

* Memorandum of the Case of the National Congress of British West Africa for a Memorial Based upon the Resolution to be Presented to His Majesty the King Emperor in Council through the Right Honourable the Secretary of State for the Colonies – London 1920.

He said that he had received private letters from some Nigerian Chiefs repudiating the 'ridiculous and pretentious' claims of the Nigerian delegates to the Conference, and assured everybody that the National Congress of British West Africa was not recognized by the Nigerian Government. The ideas of the Congress were incompatible with that natural development of real national self-government which all true patriots in Nigeria and all honest men should combine to secure and maintain. This national self-government, he declared, was government by natural rulers through indigenous institutions and in accordance with the rules laid down by the British administration.

> Assuming, therefore, for a moment that the impossible were feasible – that this collection of self-contained and mutually independent native states were indeed capable of being welded into a single homogeneous nation – a deadly blow would be struck at the very root of national self-government in Nigeria, which secures to each separate people the right to maintain its identity, its individuality and its nationality, its own chosen form of government, and the peculiar political and social institutions which have been evolved for it by the wisdom and accumulated experience of generations of its forebears.

For Clifford, Nigeria meant a collection of 'nations', ruled by a government directed from abroad.

But in spite of these strictures on the educated Nigerians of the coastal areas, the government was constrained to make some concessions to them, and within two years of the Accra Conference, a new Constitution was promulgated for Nigeria by which the elective principle was introduced, and the old deliberative and consultative Council gave way to a more broadly based Legislative Council with powers, subject to the Colonial Laws Validity Act of 1865, to make laws for the Colony and Protectorate of Southern Nigeria.

In a speech announcing the new constitutional provisions to a meeting of the Nigerian Council on 26 February 1923, the Governor commended the new Legislative Council as an institution which offered ample scope for educated Nigerians of ability to examine and criticize the government's management of public finance and to make an effective contribution in the governing of a 'united Nigeria'.

The Nigeria Protectorate Order-in-Council of 1922 provided for:

(i) The division of the Protectorate into two portions, each under a Lieutenant-Governor appointed by the Crown.

(ii) The establishment of a single Executive Council for and over the whole of the Colony and Protectorate of Nigeria.

(iii) A Legislative Council with powers and authority to make laws for maintenance of peace, order and good government in the Colony and Southern Provinces of the Protectorate.

(iv) The Governor by Ordinance to provide for the administration of justice, the raising of revenue and generally for the peace, order and good government of the Northern Provinces of the Protectorate and all persons therein, including the prohibition and punishment of all acts tending to disturb the public peace.

(v) The Governor to be empowered to apply to the Northern Provinces any ordinance passed by the Legislative Council, but this not to confer any power on the Legislative Council to make laws affecting the Northern Provinces.

The Royal Instructions which were published along with the Order-in-Council provided that the Executive Council should consist of the Chief Secretary to the Government, the Lieutenant-Governors, Administrator of the Colony, Attorney-General, Commandant of the Nigeria Regiment, Director of Medical and Sanitary Services, Treasurer, Director of Marine, Controller of Customs, Secretary for Native Affairs, Director of Education, and Director of Transport.* But the Governor was authorized to appoint up to three unofficials as members of the Council for periods of three years. The Royal Instructions also provided that the Legislative Council consist of the Governor as President, 26 official members, 3 *elected* unofficial members representing the municipal area of Lagos, 1 *elected* unofficial member representing the municipal area of Calabar, and no more than 15 nominated unofficial members.†

The qualifications for elected members and for electors were laid down by the Nigeria (Legislative Council) Order-in-Council 1922 as follows:

* Added in 1938.

† In 1928 the number of official members was increased to 30.

(i) To be eligible for election as a member of the Legislative Council a person must be a registered elector in Lagos in the case of any of the Lagos seats and a registered elector in Calabar in the case of the Calabar seat.

(ii) To be registered as an elector a person must be:

(*a*) a British subject or a 'native' of the Protectorate of Nigeria;

(*b*) 21 years of age or upwards;

(*c*) resident for the 12 months immediately preceding the date of registration in the appropriate municipal area; and

(*d*) during the calendar year immediately preceding, in possession of a gross income from all sources of not less than £100.

No person was entitled to be registered as an elector or to vote if he had been sentenced by a competent British Court, whether within or outside Nigeria, for any crime punishable by death, imprisonment with hard labour for any period, or imprisonment for any period exceeding one year, and had not received a free pardon for the crime for which he or she had been sentenced; or was of unsound mind.

In the same year as the new Constitution was being introduced, the former German Protectorate of the Cameroons was placed under British Mandate by the League of Nations. The territory became known as the Cameroons and was administered as part of Nigeria; and an Ordinance was enacted to provide for the application of most laws which were passed by the Legislative Council of the Colony and Protectorate of Nigeria to the mandated territory of the Cameroons.

The new Legislative Council was thus an advance on its predecessor. It made laws for the Colony and the Southern Provinces. Furthermore, these laws were applicable to the Northern Provinces by the special proclamation of the Governor, and because the Northern Provinces had a common annual budget with the Colony and the Southern Provinces, it was within the competence of the Legislative Council to debate government policy in the North where finance was involved. The new Council also made laws in respect of the Southern Cameroons under British Mandate.

The Order-in-Council came into force in June 1923, and elections were held in Lagos and Calabar on 20 September of the same year. At the inaugural meeting of the new Legislative Council, the Governor, Sir Hugh Clifford, told members that the Council was designed to aid and strengthen the Government in the task of administering the country. There was no question of Government and Opposition, but instead an endeavour to insure closer cooperation and sympathy between the government and the governed. The unofficial members were being brought into closer touch with the administration in order that they might have a deeper insight into local affairs, and a better understanding of the difficulties and problems of government. It was the first time in the history of the Negro peoples in Africa that the privilege of selecting their own representatives by the exercise of the franchise had been extended to any area of the continent.

This was indeed a very real advance in the constitutional history of Nigeria; but far more significant changes took place in the sphere of local government as a result of the 1922 constitution, and because these changes affected both the structure and functions of the Central Government for nearly thirty years, they deserve detailed consideration.

When Lugard became governor of the Protectorate of Northern Nigeria, he found that only by giving formal recognition to the existing political system and the rule of the Fulani Emirs could he exercise effective executive control over such a vast territory; therefore, once he subjugated each Emir, he promptly reinstated him on terms. Every Emir was handed a Staff of Office by Lugard at an installation ceremony, which left the Emir and his subjects in no doubt as to the source of his new authority. In his first annual report on the administration of Northern Nigeria, Lugard described the policy of his government as one which 'utilizes and works through the native chiefs and avails itself of the intelligence and powers of government, of the Fulani caste in particular, but insists upon their observance of the fundamental laws of humanity and justice'.

British Residents were appointed and charged with the primary responsibility of promoting this policy, which was later christened 'Indirect Rule'. If an Emir proved unamenable to the control of the protectorate government, he was deposed and replaced by a more tractable figure. The government regulated the payment of tributes by the villagers to the Emirs and prevented extortion by agents of the Emirs or any undue burden of taxation upon the peasants and the trading classes. Under Lugard's successors, 'Native Administrations' were established in all the emirates, and each Emir was formally appointed the 'Sole Native Authority'. Every Native Administration was equipped with a Treasury (into which a fixed share of the taxes collected by the protectorate government was paid), public works organization, Native Court, and local police force. The work of the Native Administration and its Court was supervised by the Resident, who was responsible to the Governor for the efficient and smooth running of the administration. On the amalgamation of the Protectorates of the North and the South, some attempt was made to introduce the Northern pattern of Native Administration into the Southern Provinces. Overami, the exiled Oba of Benin, died in 1914, and when his successor was installed in 1915, an emirate type of Native Administration was established in Benin. The experiment failed because for some twenty years, following the Benin Expedition, the kingdom of Benin had been ruled directly by British political officers, and the Chiefs had lost their influence and prestige. In 1916, however, a Native Administration was successfully established in Oyo on the basis of the 'ancient institutions which had been evolved for themselves by the political genius of the people of the Yoruba country'.

After 1922, the government of Nigeria directed its energies and resources to the setting up of Native Administrations throughout the country, and by 1945, one hundred and fourteen principal Native Authorities and several hundreds more subordinate ones had been established. In 1923, two Ordinances were enacted which provided the statutory framework for the policy of Indirect Rule throughout the country. The Native Authority Ordinance imposed upon every Native Authority the duty to maintain order and good government and to prevent the commission of any offence within its area of jurisdiction: and conferred upon it power to make Rules and Orders, providing for the

> peace, good order and welfare of all the persons within its jurisdiction; to regulate or control local trade, agriculture and land usage; to collect rates, regulate traffic, and the movement of persons within

the jurisdiction; control burial places, places of entertainment and public health generally; to declare and modify native law and custom.

A Native Authority was constituted either by one person, such as an Emir, Oba or traditional chief designated 'A Sole Native Authority', or by any group of persons appointed by the government 'in accordance with the native custom of the community concerned'.*

By the Native Courts Ordinance, and subject to the limitations imposed by the Warrant which created it, every Native Court exercised civil and criminal jurisdiction over all persons who resided within, and were subject to the jurisdiction of the Native Authority for, the area in which the Native Court was established. The Court administered the native law and custom which prevailed in that area to the extent that it was not regarded as being repugnant to natural justice and morality or inconsistent with any provisions of any Ordinance of the Government of Nigeria. The Native Court enforced the Rules and Orders made by the Native Authority of the area and any other legal provisions which the Legislative Council authorized it to enforce. Native Courts were under the control of Residents and District Officers who were empowered to review the proceedings of the Courts or sit on appeal over their decisions. Legal practitioners were not permitted to appear before the Courts to assist persons summoned before them.

The policy of Indirect Rule thus depended for its success on the existence of three factors: (1) a stratified society, consisting of a ruling aristocracy and a peasantry or rank and file of the population; (2) a degree of social immobility which prevented persons of a lower class from advancing to a higher one; and (3) some identity of interests between the ruling class and the occupying power. In principle, under the Indirect Rule system of government, British political officers themselves were supposed to perform no executive functions. They could intervene to see that the Native Authority took action where necessary without themselves taking the action. They were advisers and superintendents who left the

* By section 5 (1) of the Native Authority Ordinance 1923, the Governor might by notice in the Gazette appoint to any office of Native Authority so situated in the protectorate *(a)* any Chief or other person; *(b)* any Chief associated with a Council; *(c)* any Council; *(d)* any group of persons.

day-to-day work of administration to the control of Nigerians whose claim to authority was based on tradition. All three factors existed together in most of the emirates in the Northern Provinces. In the South it was not possible to find any two of the factors existing together anywhere. To be sure, centralized authority was a basic feature of the traditional Yoruba oligarchy, and it was therefore possible to build a sort of Indirect Rule on such foundations. East of the Niger, however, where the prevalent indigenous political system was segmentary, Indirect Rule had no meaning at all. Native Administrations were established in various districts complete with Councils, Native Courts, Treasuries and Local Works Departments; but despite all these external trappings, the District Officer was the principal executive and magisterial authority of his district. The Councils had little authority, no independence, and were reluctant to accept any financial responsibility.

In the course of time Indirect Rule, despite its failure in the South, began to be looked upon as a sacrosanct institution, handed down by divine revelation, which none but the most impious dared to criticize. It was so jealously guarded by the political officers that two parallel and almost mutually exclusive systems of government developed. And this gave rise to such farcical situations as the development of a separate 'town' in a certain Nigerian city, where the Central Government Police in the 'town' were required to abandon the pursuit of a burglar the moment he crossed the boundary into the area under the charge of the Native Authority Police, and the latter were similarly required to abandon the pursuit of a criminal who sought refuge in the area of Nigerian Police jurisdiction. With a few notable exceptions, most Native Authorities consisted of illiterate, conservative, and autocratic chiefs, who were either unwilling to move with the times or incapable of it. The younger, educated members of the community were in most cases excluded from membership of their Native Authority Councils because of the Nigerian Government's determination to perpetuate the indigenous and traditional systems of administration.

Ambitious young men outside Lagos and Calabar found all ways to public life barred except through the narrow gate of nomination into the Legislative Council. This devotion to the theory and practice of Indirect Rule not only ossified local development in Nigeria, it retarded constitutional growth for a quarter of a century. The Legislative Council which was established under the 1922 Constitution remained unchanged until the end of 1945 and, although it counted among its membership some of the most brilliant and ablest Nigerians, it soon became an anachronism by-passed by the mainstream of Nigerian nationalism. The small band of Nigerians, however honest and well-meaning, who continued to serve on the Council were dubbed 'Uncle Toms' and 'Yes-men' by the more aggressive nationalists. By 1939, political leadership in the Southern Provinces had passed from the hands of the Honourable Members of the Legislative Council to the nationalists who controlled the politically vibrant press. The Northern Provinces continued in peaceful isolation from the South, screened and sheltered from subversive outside influences by their political officers and the dogma of Indirect Rule. Their inhabitants continued for twenty-five years to be denied a voice in the highest legislature of the land and in the management of the public purse to which they contributed. It took the combined momentum of Nigerian political journalism, organized labour and a world war to move Nigeria one more step along the path of nationhood.

In March 1945, the Governor, Sir Arthur Richards (later Lord Milverton), published the substance of his Dispatch to the Secretary of State for the Colonies as 'Sessional Paper No. 4 of 1945: *Political and Constitutional Future of Nigeria*';[15] and on 22 March the Acting Chief Secretary to the Government moved the adoption of the Sessional Paper by the Legislative Council. In his introductory Speech he outlined the object and principles which were followed in framing the proposals. These, he declared, were:

(*a*) to promote the unity of Nigeria;
(*b*) to secure greater participation by Africans in their own affairs;
(*c*) to evolve a constitutional framework covering the whole of Nigeria and a Legislative Council on which all sections of Nigeria would be represented;
(*d*) to create Regional Councils in the three main sections into which Nigeria fell naturally (both politically and

constitutionally), North, West and East, under their respective Chief Commissioners;

(*e*) to forge political and constitutional links between the Native Authorities and the Legislative Council by means of a chain of representation through the Houses of Assembly in the Regions to the Central Legislative Council;

(*f*) to provide for an African majority, both in the Houses of Assembly and the Legislative Council.

The proposals were intended to be a development or upward projection of the system of Native Administration which was the adopted policy of Nigeria. It was conceded that Native Administrations had hitherto concerned themselves with purely local affairs; their interests had remained local and their connexions confined to the people of the area in which each of them operated. Native Authorities, as then constituted, were not completely representative of the people, but the basis of Native Authority Councils was in the process of being broadened to secure the participation of the educated and progressive elements in the management of local affairs, and generally to make all bodies responsible for local administration more representative of public opinion. Furthermore, in order to ensure that no section of responsible public opinion was excluded from the highest legislature of the land, representation through Native Authorities would be supplemented by the well-tried system of nomination, whereby special interests not otherwise represented would be served through persons appointed by the Governor to be members either of Regional Assemblies or the Legislative Council. The new Constitution, therefore, provided for:

1. The division of Nigeria into three Administrative Regions – Northern, Eastern and Western – each under a Chief Commissioner;

2. The establishment of an Executive Council consisting of the Chief Secretary to the Government of Nigeria; the Chief Commissioner of each of the three Regions; the Attorney General; the Financial Secretary; the Director of Medical Services; the Director of Education; and such other persons as might from time to time be appointed by the Governor

on the instructions of the Secretary of State for the Colonies;

3. A Legislative Council consisting of the Governor, (as President); 13 *ex-officio* members; 3 nominated official members; 24 nominated unofficial members; and 4 elected members. The *ex-officio* members to be the Chief Secretary, the Chief Commissioners of the three Regions, the Attorney-General, the Financial Secretary, the Director of Medical Services, Development Secretary, Director of Education, Director of Agriculture, Director of Public Works, Commissioner of Labour, Commissioner of the Colony. The nominated official members to be 3 Residents (1 from each Region) appointed by the Governor. The nominated unofficial members to be:
   (*a*) 4 members of the House of Chiefs of the Northern Provinces, appointed by the Chiefs of that House;
   (*b*) 5 members of the Northern House of Assembly appointed by the unofficial members of that House from amongst themselves;
   (*c*) 2 members appointed by the Governor from those Chiefs who were members of the Western House of Assembly;
   (*d*) 4 members, being unofficial members of the Western House of Assembly, appointed by the unofficial members of that House;
   (*e*) 5 members, being official members of the Eastern House of Assembly, appointed by unofficial members of that House;
   (*f*) 1 member for the Colony appointed by the Governor after consultation with the Native Authorities in the Colony; and
   (*g*) 3 members appointed by the Governor to represent interests of communities which, in his opinion, were not adequately represented.

   Of the 4 elected members, 3 to represent the Municipality of Lagos, and 1 the Township of Calabar.

4. A House of Chiefs and a House of Assembly for the Northern Region; and Houses of Assembly for each of the Eastern and Western Regions.

(*a*) The House of Chiefs would consist of the Chief Commissioner of the Northern Provinces as President; all first class Chiefs in the Northern Region, and not less than 10 second class Chiefs, selected from among their own members by an electoral college of second class Chiefs.

(*b*) The Northern House of Assembly would consist of the Senior Resident in the Northern Provinces as President; 12 Residents of the Northern Provinces, (including the Secretary, Northern Provinces); the Secretary for Finance, the Deputy Director of Medical Services, the Deputy Director of Education, the Deputy Director of Agriculture, the Deputy Director of Works, the Senior Crown Counsel; and not less than 20 nor more than 24 unofficial members, of whom 14 to 18 were to be selected by Native Authorities (Provincial Members), and 6 were to be appointed by the Governor to represent interests and communities which, in his opinion, were not otherwise adequately represented.

(*c*) The Western House of Assembly would consist of the Chief Commissioner of the Western Provinces as President; 7 Residents of the Western Provinces, (including the Secretary, Western Province); the Secretary for Finance, the Deputy Director of Medical Services, the Deputy Director of Education, the Deputy Director of Agriculture, the Deputy Director of Public Works, the Senior Crown Counsel; and not less than 15 nor more than 19 unofficial members, of whom 3 were to be Head Chiefs of the Western Provinces, appointed by the Governor, 7 to 11 (Provincial members) selected by Native Authorities, and 5 appointed by the Governor to represent interests and communities which, in his opinion, were not otherwise adequately represented.

(*d*) The Eastern House of Assembly would consist of the Chief Commissioner of the Eastern Provinces as President; 7 Residents of the Eastern Provinces (including the Secretary, Eastern Provinces), the Secretary for Finance, the Deputy Director of Medical Services, the Deputy Director of Education, the Deputy Director of Agriculture, the Deputy Director of Public Works, the Senior Crown Counsel; and not less than 15 nor more than 20 unofficial members, of whom 10 to 13 (Provincial members) were to be selected by Native Authorities, and five were to be appointed by the Governor to represent interests or communities which, in his opinion, were not adequately represented.

The Regional Assemblies were to function as electoral colleges for the purpose of appointing members to the Legislative Council. They were to consider and advise by resolution on any matter referred to them by the Governor or introduced by a Member of the Assembly. Estimates of Expenditure both Annual and Supplementary were to be placed before the Regional Houses, as well as any Bill whose terms were applicable to the Region concerned. In its subsequent consideration of Bills and Estimates, the Legislative Council would receive the Government's proposals as amended according to those recommendations of the Regional Houses which the Governor saw fit to adopt.

These constitutional proposals represented in some respects real constitutional progress. By bringing representatives of the Northern Provinces into an all-Nigeria Legislative Council, the new constitution encouraged a sense of common cause amongst Nigerians which had not existed before. It fostered Nigerian unity by giving every section of the country some share in policy-making and administration. By dividing Nigeria into three Regions it recognized the necessity for administrative devolution in a country the size of Nigeria, where the system of communications was very poor, and where educational and social development was uneven. Regionalism has always been regarded by many Nigerians as one of the worst features of the 1946 (Richards) Constitution; but although the Richards Constitution gave forceful constitutional validity to the administrative division of the country into three Regions, these divisions existed as far back as 1939, when the Southern Provinces were divided into the Eastern and Western Provinces under the administrative charge of two Chief Commissioners based at Enugu and Ibadan. Contrary to popular belief, the Richards Constitution did not divide Nigeria into three immutable autonomous Regions. By Section

5(1) of the Nigeria (Protectorate and Cameroons) Order-in-Council of 1946

> The Protectorate shall be divided into two regions to be known as the Northern Provinces and the Southern Provinces thereof respectively; and the Southern Provinces as aforesaid shall be divided into two regions to be known as the Western Provinces and the Eastern Provinces thereof respectively;

while by Section 5(2)

> The Governor may by proclamation with the approval of His Majesty signified through a Secretary of State define, and from time to time vary, the boundaries between any two of such regions, and further may divide all or any such regions for administrative purposes in such manner as he may consider expedient.[16]

It is submitted that this section conferred on the Governor sufficient discretionary powers to enable him to further divide the Regions as they then existed into smaller Regions.

The other positive merit of the Richards Constitution was that it widened the basis of representation in the Legislative Council. The unofficial members, although selected by Native Authorities, had direct links with the people they were chosen to represent. They were members of Native Authority Councils and not just individuals nominated by the Government to represent areas in which they had no roots.

The Nigerian reaction to the Richards Constitution varied between the extremes of uncompromising opposition and uncritical acceptance. The Government itself did not deem it necessary to consult Nigerian opinion beyond mentioning the matter to four first class Chiefs in the Western Provinces and an important Emir in the North. Not even members of the Legislative Council were consulted prior to the final formulation of the proposals, and this was – not surprisingly – regarded as a calculated insult by many Nigerians in Lagos. Unofficial members of the Legislative Council received copies of the Sessional Paper embodying the proposals a few days before the debate on it was due to take place. They held a private meeting amongst themselves and decided to ask for a postponement of the debate on the motion, but were required to consider the Sessional Paper immediately; in the event, their criticism was superficial and vain, with their complaints directed mainly against the so-called unofficial majority. Earlier in the Session the Chief Secretary to the Government had stated, in answer to a question put to him by a member of the Council, that 'Native Authorities are indigenous institutions which the Government has recognized and to which it has assigned definite powers and allotted definite duties, the principal of which are set out in the Native Authority and Direct Taxation Ordinances.' Native Authorities were an integral part of the machinery of Government, he declared, a machinery which had been designed with the very definite aim of educating the people of the country politically and administratively, in order that they might gradually take a larger and larger part in the management of their own affairs. It was, therefore, incomprehensible to members that a majority which included four Emirs and two Obas (all first class Chiefs) should pass by the name of an 'unofficial majority'. There was also some rather desultory criticism of the Government's decision not to extend the elective principle to urban communities besides Lagos and Calabar, and of the proposal that there should not be 'any change in the constitution of the Executive Council, the functions of which are purely advisory, and which has recently been enlarged by the addition of three unofficial members'. At the time of this debate there were two Nigerian unofficial members in the Executive Council, neither of whom was a member of the Legislative Council. Some members noted the 'break in the link between the Legislative Council and the Executive Council', but the matter was not seriously argued, and at the end of the debate the constitutional proposals were unanimously adopted by the African unofficial members of the Legislative Council.

While these Nigerians were restrained in their criticisms of the new constitution, however, the press was violent in its condemnation, and the legislators were castigated for supporting the proposals without first consulting the country. Apart from the indignation against the Government for forcing an 'undemocratic constitution' on the people, there was discontent with the method of nomination to the Legislative Council; selection to the Regional Assemblies through the Native Authorities; the phoney unofficial majority; and the repudiation by the Government of the elective principle and universal adult suffrage. Yet, despite the storm of protests and resolutions, new Letters Patent, Orders-in-Council and Royal Instructions were published; Native Authorities in each Province selected from among their own members representatives to attend the meetings held for the purpose of selecting the provincial members of the Houses of Assembly; and the latter at their first meeting selected some of their own number to be members of the Legislative Council. Elections were also held in Lagos and Calabar to choose the four elected members.

Nowhere in Nigeria was opposition to the Richards Constitution as strong as in Lagos, and the Nigerian National Democratic Party under the sponsorship of the N.C.N.C. (at that time a united front of all political elements) won all the three Lagos seats in the Legislative Council on the promise that it would fight for the immediate repeal of the Richards Constitution. The Governor was displeased.

> I am becoming increasingly conscious of the cleavage of interest and outlook between Lagos and the rest of Nigeria – perhaps I ought to say between Nigeria and Lagos. Inside government service, the accusation has often been made that the Central Government is too much coloured by residence in Lagos, and that to view Nigeria through Lagos spectacles is to have a distorted and false view. If there are any grounds for such an opinion inside of the Government whose officers are constantly renewed from the Provinces, and sent out again to the Provinces, how much more must it be true of those who live always in Lagos and claim a Nigerian mandate on the strength of plaudits of the unemployed who flood the overcrowded streets of the capital and form one of its chief problems.*

But the three Lagos seats were won not by the votes of the unemployed, for they had none. They were won by the votes of those residents of Lagos who qualified by possessing a 'gross annual income of not less than fifty pounds' – a respectable sum in the 1940s. And the political leaders chosen for the Lagos seats had not only the mandate of the people of Lagos, but the mandates and monies of thousands of Nigerian communities and individuals, in support of their delegation to the Colonial Office in 1947 to demand the repeal of the Richards Constitution.

The Constitution undoubtedly had its merits, principal among

* Speech and Address of His Excellency Sir Arthur Richards to the Legislative Council, 18 March 1946, Government Printer, Lagos, 1946.

which was the establishment of an all-Nigeria Legislature. But it was ten years late both in timing and method of presentation. It was inevitable that the Second World War, the Atlantic Charter and the events in India and Burma, where thousands of Nigerian soldiers saw active military service, should have their impact on Nigerian opinion even far out in the villages. The system of Native Administration as it existed in 1945 was quite unable to meet the requirements of an efficiently developing democratic administration. Efforts had been made here and there to accommodate the younger and more educated elements in Native Authority Councils, but the core of these Councils remained illiterate and traditionalist, the staff inadequately trained and poorly paid, and their executive functions still largely performed by District Officers. This was an inappropriate foundation upon which to build the superstructure of a national legislature. Contrary to the expressed intentions of the Government, a constitution based on such traditional authorities could not contain within it the living possibilities of expansion and development. No doubt, the traditional system of self-government was well adapted to the habits and thoughts of the people at a particular point in history, but that point was long past by 1945. And the refusal to associate Nigerians with the executive side of government was perhaps even more serious a mistake. There could have been no more effective way of securing greater participation by Africans in the discussion and management of their own affairs than that of bringing them into the Executive Council, where government policy was formulated and the final decision was taken on what advice to give the Governor on any particular matter.

Sir Arthur Richards (now Lord Milverton) is still remembered in Nigeria as the man who introduced Regionalism. Indeed, he was a stout advocate of the principle of 'unity in diversity'. But his policy of regionalization was directed more to administrative devolution than to political separation of the various groups in the country. Although most departments of government were regionalized, central direction and coordination still remained with the Secretariat in Lagos. It was the Nigerians who were themselves largely the architects of the schism that threatened national unity.

4. Nationalism: Its Growth and Development

Nigerian nationalism began as a protest movement. It arose soon after the First World War from the desire of the small group of British-educated Nigerians to participate in the public affairs of the Colony, and to be accorded greater social recognition by the colonial civil servants. In 1920 some Nigerian lawyers, doctors and merchants from Lagos and Calabar participated in a conference held in Accra, Gold Coast, by a body known as the National Congress of British West Africa. The purpose of the conference was in the words of its Chairman, 'not to organize any anti-government movement but to help the work of the government in a loyal and constitutional manner'. During a week-long meeting the conference resolved:

(i) That no important measures affecting the people must be passed without the consent and direct cooperation of the chiefs and people.
(ii) That the principle whereby the Governor nominates unofficial members of the Legislative Council is suspect and should be abolished and in its place should be substituted the principle of enfranchisement of the people.
(iii) That this congress views with great disfavour the propaganda of the Empire Resources Development Committee which regards the natural resources of the British West African Colonies as free property for exploitation by British concessionaires under state protection.
(iv) That this conference deplores the activities of the Empire Resources Development Committee which threaten to reduce British West African farmers to conditions which prevailed in pre-war German Colonies where the African was reduced to the position of serf on his own soil for the benefit of European exploiters.
(v) That the Public Lands Acquisition Ordinances by which West

African Governments acquire land compulsorily on payment of a nominal compensation and afterwards let the same land to private companies at higher rents should be modified in order to give the owners of the land the benefits of the bargain.

(vi) That this Congress demands that the discriminatory practices which now exist in the West African Civil Service should be abolished and that all appointments be made subject to merit and not by reason of colour, race or creed. In this connexion, it is important to remember the Proclamation of Her late Majesty Queen Victoria: 'And it is our further will that, as far as may be, our subjects of whatever race or creed, be freely and impartially admitted to office in our Service, the duties of which they may be qualified by their education, ability and integrity to discharge.'

(vii) That this Congress views with alarm the right assumed by European Powers to exchange or partition countries between themselves without reference to, or regard for, the wishes of the people. Such a course of action is tantamount to a species of slavery. Congress strongly condemns the partitioning of Togoland and Cameroons between the British and French Governments.

(viii) That this congress believes that the time has now come to found a British West African University on such lines as would preserve in the students a sense of African Nationality.

These resolutions were embodied in a memorial submitted to the King through the Secretary of State for the Colonies.[17]

One outcome of the Accra Conference was the emergence between 1920 and 1922 of two political parties in Lagos – the Nigerian National Democratic Party and the People's Union – to contest elections for the new Legislative Council which was established in 1923. But these parties were neither national nor democratic. The majority of their members were doctors, lawyers and prosperous businessmen from the leading Lagos families, completely out of touch with the needs of the mass of the people in Lagos and the rest of the country, and they neither sought nor received popular support. The parties did not put forward any positive political, economic or social programme. Their influence remained negative, the membership small and their interests sectional. For nearly two decades the tide of nationalism ebbed. Then in 1937, the deteriorating economic situation in Nigeria rekindled the nationalist fire. In that year the European Produce Trading Firms organized a price-fixing ring for the cocoa trade, called the 'West African Cocoa Pool'. The reaction of the African middlemen in the cocoa trade throughout West Africa was both hostile and spontaneous. The middlemen organized a boycott of European firms which were members of the Cocoa Pool, and sent a delegation to the Colonial Office in London to demand British Government protection of African commercial interests from the monopoly of the Cocoa Pool. In Nigeria, the agitation against the Cocoa Pool was led by a political association known as the Nigerian Youth Movement.

This association originally came into existence in 1934 as the Lagos Youth Movement, to protest against the establishment by the Nigerian Government of a post-secondary educational institution in Lagos, the Higher College Yaba. The Government's aim was to provide some professional training locally to satisfy the intermediate manpower requirements of the public service. The College offered diploma courses in medicine, engineering, agriculture, forestry, commerce, natural science and humanities. The professional elite in Lagos protested vehemently against the local production of 'half-baked' professional men to compete with them. In this protest the artisans, clerical workers and non-graduate teachers made common cause with the elite because they believed that the new cadre of public servants trained at Yaba constituted a threat to their prospects of advancement in the service. Although initially the protest was motivated by professional and occupational jealousies, it quickly assumed a political complexion and under the new name of the Nigerian Youth Movement the association became the political platform for the fight against imperialism, economic exploitation and social inequality. By 1938, the Youth Movement had recruited into its ranks many of the products of Yaba who were themselves smarting under the humiliation of a Yaba Diploma which, although it was of high professional standard, condemned its holder to an inferior status in the public service. The Nigerian Youth Movement, unlike its predecessors the Democratic Party and the People's Union, established branches in many of the urban centres in the southern portion of the country; and in both the Local and Legislative Council Elections which took place in Lagos in 1938 it won all the seats from the Democratic Party which was until then the only political party represented in the

Legislature. The Youth Movement had as its objectives;

> the unification of the different tribes of Nigeria by adopting and encouraging means which will foster better understanding and cooperation between the tribes so that they may come to have a common ideal; complete autonomy for Nigeria within the British Empire and economic opportunities equal to those enjoyed by foreigners.

The growth of nationalism during the years preceding the Second World War was stimulated by two other factors: the development of an indigenous newspaper industry and the emergence of the 'Tribal Improvement Unions'.

In 1937, Mr Nnamdi Azikiwe (as he then was) established the *West African Pilot* in Lagos, and the following year the Nigerian Youth Movement began to publish a newsheet, the *Service*, which was later converted to a daily newspaper called the *Daily Service*. These two papers devoted most of their columns to uninhibited political propaganda against colonialism. Dr Azikiwe propounded from day to day the principles of his political and economic philosophy which he described as 'African irridentism, political risorgimento and economic determinism'. Both newspapers daily dramatized the political, economic and social disabilities imposed upon Nigerians by the colonial administration; and urged Nigerian Youth to acquire political education and national consciousness to enable them to 'throw off the shackles of imperialism' at the earliest possible moment.

The Tribal Improvement Unions came into prominence about the same time as the Nigerian-owned press. As their name suggests, their original purpose was the social improvement of their respective tribal areas. Their members were the young men and women who migrated from the rural areas to take up paid employment in the urban centres. First, they gathered together on Sunday afternoons to entertain themselves. Then they began to think of improvements for their villages. They believed education to be the greatest single benefit they could confer on their people; so they taxed themselves to raise money to award scholarships to their 'deserving youth' to acquire secondary and overseas university education. As the influence of the unions grew they began to act as 'pressure groups' in the affairs of their local administration. They organized press campaigns to focus the attention of the government on the social needs of their respective tribal areas, including the demand for better roads, dispensaries and maternity hospitals. Later the Unions became active propagandists for the nationalist movement in the demand for self-government.

When the Second World War broke out in 1939, anti-colonial political propaganda temporarily ceased. Instead the newspapers and nationalist leaders gave full support to the British war effort and urged young Nigerians to enlist in the army. They encouraged the 'Win the War' campaigns which were organized throughout the country to raise funds for the war and assured the people that Nigeria's prospects of self-government were far better under the British than under the Germans. Many Nigerians enlisted in the West African Frontier Force and participated in the campaigns in North and East Africa and in Burma and India. Service overseas broadened the political outlook of many of the troops; but more particularly, the war propaganda of the Western democracies stimulated discussion about self-determination. During the critical years of the war Nigeria assumed an important strategic position for the Western Allies; and it was the base from which thousands of European and American servicemen reached the Middle East. Therefore, Nigerians came into contact with thousands of foreigners and had access to the publications of the Army Bureau of Current Affairs and the Fabian Society, all of which extolled the virtues of parliamentary democracy and the principle of self-determination. There was some official effort to arouse expectations of major political advance once the war was successfully concluded. These events were not lost on Nigerians. The declaration of the Atlantic Charter by President Roosevelt and Mr Winston Churchill in August 1942 was the signal for the new marching order. A few days after the historic declaration, Clement Attlee, as Deputy Prime Minister, assured a Conference of the West African Students' Union in London that Africans were as much entitled to the benefits of the Atlantic Charter as any other nation on earth. On reading about Attlee's statement, Dr Nnamdi Azikiwe, then one of the leaders of the Nigerian Youth Movement, cabled Churchill, requesting him to give official confirmation to the statement in order to stimulate the African war effort in support of the Anglo-American Alliance.

In an evasive reply Churchill all but repudiated Attlee's statement; but in spite of this repudiation the West African Students' Union adopted a resolution demanding 'Internal self-government for West Africa immediately and complete independence in five years'. This resolution marked the beginning of a new phase of nationalism in Nigeria. It was no longer a protest against racial contempt and economic exploitation, but a struggle for national self-determination. All sections of the community continued to support the British war effort but the issue of self-determination was now uppermost in the minds of the educated youth, particularly in Lagos. The activities of the All-India Congress were followed with considerable interest and the need for a National Front was publicly canvassed by the various youth study groups which emerged during that period – the Nigerian Reconstruction Group, the Nigerian Youth Circle and the Nigerian Union of Students – all of which were concerned with the 'study of Nigerian social problems with a view to offering well-informed and authoritative criticism of government policies and programmes'. Through the activities of these Youth groups the National Council of Nigeria and the Cameroons (N.C.N.C.) was inaugurated in Lagos in August 1944. The new organization aimed:

> to extend democratic principles and to advance the interests of the people of Nigeria and the Cameroons under British Mandate; to organize and collaborate with all its branches throughout the country; to adopt suitable means for the purpose of imparting political education to the people of Nigeria with a view to achieving self-government; to afford the members the advantages of a medium of expression in order to secure political freedom, economic security, social equality and religious toleration in Nigeria and the Cameroons under British Mandate, as a member of the British Commonwealth of Nations.

At its inception, the N.C.N.C. was not a political party. It was conceived as a united National Front embracing all nationalist political groups which agitated for self-government. Accordingly, the existing political parties – the Nigerian National Democratic Party and the Nigerian Youth Movement – and the politically-oriented youth associations became members of the Council. Herbert Macauley, a veteran politician and Leader of the Nigerian National Democratic Party, was elected President, Dr Nnamdi Azikiwe, Secretary, and Dr Olorun-Nimbe, Treasurer. These three names drew massive support from a wide assortment of organizations – political, commercial, occupational and tribal. By 1945, groups as different in purpose as the Lagos Aboriginal Society, the Market Women's Association, the Ibo Union, the Railway Workers' Union, the Postal Workers' Union, and the Nigerian Ex-Servicemen's Association had become members of the N.C.N.C. This popular support proved to be both the strength and weakness of the Council: the strength because the Council indeed represented the overwhelming majority of the people in the South and some of the people in the North; the weakness because ethnic affinity had been made a basis of political action with the result that conflicts between individual Nigerians who belonged to different ethnic groups were carried over into political life and thus constituted a major obstacle to national unity.

At the end of the war when the Richards Constitution was introduced by the Governor and its provisions found to fall far short of the expectations of the younger people, the widespread disillusionment and bitterness found its spearhead in the N.C.N.C. leaders' proposal to send a delegation to the Colonial Office in London to demand the abrogation of the Richards Constitution and the grant of self-government. A section of the membership (the leaders of the Nigerian Youth Movement) opposed the proposal, arguing that the fight for self-government would be more effective if carried out within Nigeria. When they lost the argument they withdrew from the Council.

The country-wide tour the Council organized to raise funds and obtain the mandate of the people to demand self-government collected some £13,000 and hundreds of written mandates from all over the country. More important still was the return to the Legislative Council in the elections held in August 1946 of the three N.C.N.C.-sponsored candidates in all three elective seats for Lagos. A delegation was dispatched to London in the summer of 1947. The Secretary of State for the Colonies (Arthur Creech-Jones) advised the delegation to go back to Nigeria and cooperate in working the Richards Constitution. This advice caused even greater public resentment in Nigeria, and dissension among the leaders of the N.C.N.C. The personal bitterness between the leaders who belonged to different linguistic groups exacerbated the growing tribal consciousness in the country and weakened the effectiveness of the United Front. At that stage, the N.C.N.C. decided to become a political party based on individual membership rather than a united front of all the political parties. At the same time the young extremists within the ranks of the N.C.N.C. formed the 'Zikist Movement' whose aim was to pursue the political goal of self-government by 'positive Action'. During the period between August 1947, when the N.C.N.C. delegation to the Colonial Office returned to Nigeria, and the latter half of 1949, the Nationalist Movement dissipated its energies in personal rivalries and inter-tribal recriminations.

On November 1949 a tragic police shooting incident occurred at the Nigerian colliery in Enugu, where some 5,000 coal miners staged a week-long 'go-slow' strike to enforce their claim for higher wages. The incident triggered off widespread disturbances in various parts of the Eastern provinces of Nigeria. What started as a purely industrial dispute quickly became political agitation. This incident provided another opportunity for the warring nationalists to come together to form a National Emergency Committee, first to plead the cause of the miners before a Commission of Enquiry appointed to investigate the disorders, and later to present a united front in the fight for self-government; but soon after the sitting of the Commission the National Emergency Committee collapsed.

This Committee was the last serious effort to organize a united nationalist front. After 1949, the attempts by the Governors and the Legislative Council to improve on the Richards Constitution (see next chapter) convinced Nigerians of all political shades that self-government was the ultimate goal of British policy in Nigeria. Political activity was therefore directed at the time-table for self-government, and at the constitutional and administrative arrangements which would ensure a stable self-governing country. New political parties emerged in 1951 on the eve of a new constitution which introduced a ministerial system of government – the 'Action Group' in Western Nigeria and the 'Northern People's Congress' and 'Northern Elements' Progressive Union' in Northern Nigeria. All these parties accepted the goal of self-government within the Commonwealth and differed about the timing of self-government only until 1958, when they agreed on 1960 as the target date for Independence.

5. Constitutional Evolution (1948–63)

The road to federalism and independence

Shortly after launching the new Constitution in 1946 Sir Arthur Richards retired from the governorship of Nigeria, to be succeeded by Sir John Macpherson. Even so, before he left the country, he made some attempt to plug the worst leaks in the 'Richards' Constitution. In all three Regions the practice was introduced early in 1948 whereby Committees of unofficial members from each House of Assembly cooperated with the civil service departmental heads both in matters affecting legislation and in the executive actions of government.[18] At the Second Session of the Legislative Council in August 1948, Sir John Macpherson, the new Governor, announced that although it had originally been intended that the Richards Constitution would remain in force for nine years and would be reviewed at the end of that period (though limited changes might be made at the end of the third and sixth years), the progress already made in two years had been so rapid and so sound that he proposed the introduction of changes during the second three-year period. He suggested that after a period of preliminary discussions, a Select Committee of the Legislative Council should be set up, following the Budget Session of the Council in 1949, to review the whole position and to make recommendations. Accordingly, in March 1949, the Legislative Council, meeting at Ibadan, resolved that a Select Committee of the Council be set up to make recommendations to the Governor for a review of the Constitution, with special reference to the methods to be adopted for ascertaining the views of all sections of the population on the issues involved.[19]

The Select Committee, comprising all unofficial members of the Council, was subsequently appointed in terms of the resolution, and recommended that consultation of Nigerian opinion should start with discussions at village and district meetings, to be followed by Conferences at three levels – Provincial, Regional, and finally General (the representatives of the three Regions and of Lagos and the Colony). These Conferences were held throughout 1949. Provincial Conferences considered the views formulated at village and district meetings as well as memoranda and representations submitted by 'Tribal Improvement Unions' and political pressure groups. The views formulated at Provincial Conferences were then considered at Regional Conferences (including Conferences for Lagos and the Colony), and the conclusions of the Regional Conferences were incorporated in a series of resolutions which were later submitted to a Drafting Committee set up by the Select Committee of the Legislative Council.

The Regional recommendations were remarkable for their wide range of unanimity on the general principles of the constitutional framework. All the Regional Conferences recommended that constitutional advance should be based on a federal system of government and that the existing three Regional groupings (North, East and West) should be the basis of that system. They were also unanimous that the Regions should be vested with both legislative and executive authority over a wide range of subjects; that membership of both central and Regional legislatures should be by some form of election; that official representation in the legislatures and executive councils should be reduced and elected representation increased. But while the East and West wanted the establishment of Regional Executive Councils with majorities of Nigerian members and a ministerial system, the North recommended that the Chief Commissioner of each Region should exercise 'original executive powers' in all matters on which the Regional legislature had legislative competence. The Chief Commissioner would be advised by a 'Regional Executive Council' of officials and unofficials selected by him in his discretion. The Council would be solely advisory, and the Chief Commissioner would not be bound to accept its advice, although he must report to the Governor whenever he had cause to reject it, giving his reasons.

The East and West recommended a central legislature consisting largely of elected representatives and a limited number of officials; and a central Executive Council with a majority of elected members (including a limited number of officials) vested with ministerial functions. The North, while desiring a greatly enlarged central legislature, wanted no change in the purely advisory nature of the Central Executive Council. Thus, the argument about the extent to which executive functions should be transferred from British officials to elected Nigerian representatives became the central issue of the General Conference on the Review of the Constitution in January 1950, and, incidental to it, the question of Regional representation in the central legislature.

It should be recorded, however, that many young Nigerians were apprehensive of the incipient centrifugal tendencies which had been nursed by the Richards Constitution and of the growing antagonisms which were developing between North and South, Ibo and Yoruba, nationalists and legislators. Many of them attributed these antagonisms to the constitutional arrangements which facilitated the growth of Regional loyalties at the expense of national consciousness, and their apprehensions were expressed in resolutions submitted by various groups to the General Conference urging the return to unitary government. The Nigeria Society, a group of serious-minded and well-informed students in London, submitted a well-reasoned memorandum* to the Ibadan General Conference. This urged that the aim of the constitutional changes should be:

(i) the progressive transfer of executive control over Nigerian affairs to elected representatives of the people of Nigeria, and the ultimate achievement of complete self-government;
(ii) the development of a stable and united Nigeria within which the various ethnic groups would exercise the maximum control over their domestic affairs without prejudice to the good governance and security of the country as a whole; and
(iii) the forging of a common and abiding loyalty to the political

* Memorandum of the Nigeria Society to the General Conference on the Nigeria Constitution (unpublished), 1949

The present writer was Secretary of the Society. Three of the members of the Constitutional Review Study Group appointed by the Head of the Federal Military Government after the 1966 military coup were signatories to this memorandum.

entity called Nigeria, 'a loyalty which must transcend all local attachments and sectarian alignments'.

The Society proposed that these objectives would be achieved by the division of Nigeria into nine administrative units, to be called Provinces: (1) Lagos, (2) South-West, (3) Mid-West, (4) East, (5) South-East, (6) East-Central, (7) North-East, (8) North-Central and (9) North-West. This proposal was based on the belief that such a structural arrangement would minimize the dangers of the centrifugal pressures promoted by the division of Nigeria into three large units. National consciousness would be less difficult to build if none of the component units was large enough to threaten the Central Government, and Central Government control and regulation of economic policies would be facilitated. Needless to say the memorandum did not receive the attention it deserved and, although the Mid-West delegates to the General Conference indicated interest in this structural arrangement, they deferred to majority opinion. After a prolonged debate the Conference adopted a compromise proposal which recommended that the Central Executive, which should be known as the Council of Ministers, consist of:

(*a*) the Governor, as President;
(*b*) the Chief Secretary, the Financial Secretary, the Attorney-General and the three Lieutenant-Governors (the new name for the former Chief Commissioners);
(*c*) 12 elected unofficial members to be called Ministers, 4 being elected from each Region.

The Ministers would not be political or executive heads of government departments or Ministries, but would be responsible for groups of subjects. There were to be no Ministries. Each Minister would be responsible for:

(i) the initiation of discussion of policy in the Council;
(ii) introducing into the House of Representatives, and answering for therein, all business affecting his subject or group of subjects;
(iii) ensuring, in cooperation with the executive head of the Department or Departments concerned, that the decisions of the Council, as they affect his subject, are carried out.[20]

Similar arrangements were recommended for the Regional Executive Councils.

Under the new Constitution, the provisions of which were embodied in the Nigeria Constitutional Order-in-Council of 1951, the three Regions were no longer merely administrative units of government. Each Region was a political entity vested with executive and legislative powers, the limits of which were not clearly defined. The Northern and Western legislatures each consisted of a House of Chiefs and a House of Assembly, and the Eastern legislature of a House of Assembly alone. A new central legislature, re-named the House of Representatives, replaced the old Legislative Council, and direct election to the central legislature was abolished. Instead, the Regional legislatures became electoral colleges for the selection of members of the House of Representatives. Official and 'special' representation was considerably reduced.

In the North, the House of Chiefs consisted of 30 members, and the House of Assembly of 90. In the West, the House of Chiefs consisted of 20 members, and the House of Assembly of 80. In the East, the House of Assembly consisted of 84 members. The House of Representatives consisted of 136 elected members and 6 officials.

The legislature of each Region was empowered to make laws for the peace, order and good government of the Region with respect to agriculture, animal health, fisheries, forestry, local industries, cooperative societies, social welfare, education, land, regional public works, town and country planning, local government, native courts, health, regional finance, and any other matter which was within the competence of the legislature of the Region by virtue of a declaration made under Section 92 of the Nigeria (Constitution) Order-in-Council of 1951. Section 92 empowered the central legislature to delegate to a Region power to make laws with respect to any matter within the competence of the central legislature without abridging the power of the central legislature to legislate in such matter. The Lieutenant-Governor of each Region was required to send every Bill passed by the Regional legislature to the Governor. The Governor could object to any such Bill on the grounds that it:

(*a*) related to any matter with respect to which the legislature of the Region had no power;

(*b*) was inconsistent with the general interest of Nigeria or with any directions given under Section 121 of the Order-in-Council*;

or

(*c*) that it was inconsistent with the obligations of Nigeria under any treaty or other agreement.

If the Governor did not object to a Bill which was sent to him by the Lieutenant-Governor of a Region, he was required to notify the Lieutenant-Governor in writing to that effect. And thereafter the latter was empowered to assent to the Bill on behalf of the Crown. If the Governor objected to the Bill, he either returned it together with a statement of the required amendments, or with a notice that the objections could not be removed by amendment. In the former case, the Bill was sent back to the Regional legislature for amendment before being passed into law; and in the latter, it lapsed upon receipt of the Governor's notice. Any law assented to by the Lieutenant-Governor of a Region could, under section 102 of the 1951 Order-in-Council, be disallowed by the Secretary of State for the Colonies, in which case such law ceased to have effect immediately. The House of Representatives was empowered to make laws for the peace, order and good government of the whole of Nigeria. Its legislative powers were concurrent with those of the Regional legislatures in those matters in which the Region had legislative competence.

The legislative competence of the House of Representatives was restricted for Bills which related to public revenues and the public service, and by the Governor's reserved powers. By Section 84 of the Order-in-Council the House of Representatives could not proceed upon any Bill, Motion or Petition which would 'dispose of or charge any public revenue or public funds or revoke or alter any disposition thereof or charge thereon, or impose, alter or repeal any rate, tax or duty' except upon the recommendation or the consent of the Governor. By Section 85, if the Governor or

* Section 121 of the Nigeria (Constitution) Order-in-Council, 1951 provided that the Governor might from time to time give to the Lieutenant-Governor of a Region, such directions with respect to the exercise of the Executive authority of the Region as he might think desirable, and in particular might give such directions for the purpose of ensuring that the Executive authority of a Region should be so exercised as not to impede or prejudice the exercise of the Executive authority of Nigeria.

the Attorney-General gave notice to the House of Representatives that, in his opinion, a Bill or motion which was before the Houns would affect any alteration in the salary, allowances or conditioin of service (including leave, passages and promotion) of any public officer, or in the law, regulations or practice governing the payment of pensions, gratuities or other like benefits to such officer or his widow, children, dependents, or personal representatives then, except the Governor gave his consent, no further proceedings could be taken on the Bill or motion, and any action taken on it before the notice from the Governor or the Attorney-General automatically ceased to have any effect.

Finally, by Section 86, if the Governor considered that it was expedient in the interest of

> public order, public faith or good government (which expressions . . . include the responsibility of Nigeria as a territory within the British Commonwealth of Nations, and all matters pertaining to the creation and abolition of any public officer) that any Bill introduced, or any motion proposed, in the House of Representatives should have effect, then if the House fail to pass such Bill or to carry such motion within such time and in such form as the Governor may think reasonable and expedient, the Governor may at any time declare that such Bill or motion shall have effect as if it had been passed or carried by the House of Representatives.

The Lieutenant-Governor of every Region exercised similar powers in respect of Bills and motions introduced in the Regional legislature.

The Governor assented to central Bills passed by the House of Representatives on behalf of the Crown; but any law to which the Governor has given his assent could be disallowed by the Secretary of State for the Colonies. By Section 89 every Bill which was to be introduced in the House of Representatives, except an Appropriation Bill, had first to be laid upon the table of each Regional legislative house, which might then by resolution tender advice to the Governor. Bills which did not apply to a Region or were of a formal nature or were too urgent to permit of their consideration by Regional houses were, however, exempted from this provision.

A further complication in the relation between the Central and Regional legislatures was introduced by Section 107, which provided that where a Regional law was inconsistent with a Central law then:

(*a*) if the Central law was enacted before the Regional, the Regional law shall prevail and the Central law shall, to the extent of the inconsistency, be void.

(*b*) if the Central law was enacted after the Regional law, the Central law shall prevail and the Regional shall, to the extent of the inconsistency, be void.[21]

Section 118(2) provided that 'the Legislative Houses of every Region shall be deemed to be dissolved upon a dissolution of the House of Representatives.'[22] This meant that in the event of a deadlock in a Regional House, such as occurred in the Eastern House of Assembly early in 1953, all that the Lieutenant-Governor was empowered to do was discontinue meetings without dissolving the House until the five-year period which was the statutory life of the House was over or the Governor dissolved the House of Representatives under Section 117(1) of the Order-in-Council. The constitutional provision regarding the exercise of executive functions also gave cause for conflicts between the Centre and the Regions.

Sections 123 and 124 of the Order-in-Council provided for the constitution of the Executive Council in each Region. The Executive Council was the principal instrument of policy in and for each Region over matters to which the executive authority of the Region extended: the Lieutenant-Governor was obliged to consult with the Executive Council in the exercise of all powers conferred upon him by the Order, except in respect of powers which he was expressly directed or empowered to exercise in his discretion; and to act in accordance with the advice of the Council in every matter on which he was obliged to consult with the Council.

The Executive Council of the Northern Region consisted of (*a*) the Lieutenant-Governor (who was the President of the Council); (*b*) 3 *ex-officio* members (the Civil Secretary, Financial Secretary and Legal Secretary); (*c*) 2 other senior officials, i.e. Residents; and (*d*) 7 Regional Ministers, of whom 2 were members of the House of Chiefs, and 6 members of the Northern House of Assembly. In the Western Region the Executive Council consisted of (*a*) the Lieutenant-Governor as President; (*b*) 3 *ex-officio* members (the Civil Secretary, Financial Secretary and Legal Secretary); (*c*) 2 Senior Residents; and (*d*) 9 Regional Ministers, of whom 2 were members of the Western House of Assembly. The Executive Council of the Eastern Region consisted of (*a*) the Lieutenant-Governor as President; (*b*) 3 *ex-officio* members (the Civil Secretary, Financial Secretary and Legal Secretary); (*c*) 2 Senior Residents; and (*d*) 7 Regional Ministers from among the elected members of the Eastern House of Assembly.*

The procedure for appointing Regional Ministers was laid down in Section 128 of the Constitution.

(i) The Lieutenant-Governor submitted to a meeting of the House the name of the person whom he proposed for such appointment, and the unofficial members of the House decided by secret ballot whether or not to approve of the appointment. If a majority of the members present voted in favour of the person proposed, the Lieutenant-Governor appointed him by Instrument under the Public Seal of the Region.

By Section 130 (1)

(*a*) A Regional Legislative House from among the members of which a Regional Minister has been appointed may, by resolution in favour of which there are cast the votes of not less than two-thirds of all the members of the House, request the Lieutenant-Governor to revoke the appointment of such Regional Minister;

(*b*) If a Regional Legislative House, in accordance with the provisions of subsection (1) of this Section, requests the Lieutenant-Governor to revoke the appointment of a Regional Minister, the Lieutenant-Governor shall, by instrument under the Public Seal of the Region, revoke such appointment and thereupon the

* In order to resolve the deadlock which occurred in the Eastern House of Assembly in February 1953, resulting in the Lieutenant-Governor having to use his reserved powers to pass the Regional Appropriation Bill, the House of Representatives in March 1953 adopted a Central Government Motion praying the Queen to amend Section 118(1) of the Constitutional Order-in-Council so as to confer upon the Lieutenant-Governor of a Region the power to dissolve a Regional House at any time before its full five-year term and to permit of such dissolution taking place independently of the House of Representatives and the other Regional Houses. The relevant amendment was effected by Her Majesty in Council, and the Eastern House of Assembly was dissolved on 5 May 1953.

> seat of such Regional Minister in the Executive Council shall become vacant;

and by Section 130(2)

> If the Lieutenant-Governor of a Region considers that any Regional Minister has failed to carry out the policy or any decision of the Executive Council of the Region, he may . . . revoke the appointment of such Regional Minister and thereupon the seat of such Regional Minister in the Executive Council of the Region shall become vacant.

Finally, by Section 131(2)

> A Regional Minister may, by writing to the Governor, resign his seat in the Executive Council of a Region, and upon receipt of such resignation by the Lieutenant-Governor the seat of such Regional Minister shall become vacant.

The principal instrument of policy for the whole of Nigeria was the Council of Ministers, which consisted of the Governor as President, 6 *ex-officio* members and 12 elected Ministers.

The *ex-officio* members were the Chief Secretary to the Government of Nigeria, the Lieutenant-Governors of the Northern, Western and Eastern Regions, the Attorney-General, and the Financial Secretary to the Government of Nigeria. Of the 12 Ministers, 4 each were appointed from among the members of the House of Representatives returned by each of the three Regional legislatures.

For the appointment of a Minister from among members of the House of Representatives returned by any Region, the Lieutenant-Governor submitted to the Governor the name of any person whom the Lieutenant-Governor recommended for such appointment, and having considered the name so submitted, the Governor then proposed to the Lieutenant-Governor that he intended to appoint the person a Minister. In the case of Central Ministers from the Northern and Western Regions, the Lieutenant-Governor submitted the name of the person proposed by the Governor to a meeting of the Joint Council of the Region (unofficial members of the Houses of Chiefs and Assembly) to decide by secret ballot whether or not to approve of the appointment of such member. If the Joint Council approved by a simple majority vote, the Governor appointed the member a Minister by instrument under the Public Seal of Nigeria. In the case of a Central Minister from the Eastern Region the procedure differed only to the extent that the name proposed by the Governor was put to the Eastern House of Assembly in place of the Joint Council. A Central Minister could be removed from office by a resolution of the House of Representatives requesting the Governor to revoke the Minister's appointment, provided that the resolution was supported by at least two-thirds of all the members of the House. Further, the Governor could revoke the appointment of a Minister if the Minister failed to carry out the policy or any decision of the Council of Ministers, or if he ceased to be a member of the House of Representatives, or absented himself from Nigeria without written permission from the Governor, or was too ill to discharge the functions of his office. Finally, a Minister could, 'by writing under his hand addressed to the Governor resign his seat in the Council'.

Apart from their collective responsibility for the formulation of government policy, each Minister by Sections 162 and 163 had the special responsibility of (*a*) submitting in the Council of Ministers questions relating to any matter assigned to him by the Governor; (*b*) ensuring, in association with the appropriate public officer, that effect was given to the decisions taken by the Governor in the Council of Ministers relating to such matter; and (*c*) conducting in the House of Representatives government business relating to such matter. Within each Region, Regional Ministers exercised similar functions in respect of matters to which the executive authority of the Region extended, but by Section 164(2) the responsibility of a Central Minister in charge of matters within Regional competence did not extend to the function of ensuring, in association with the appropriate public officer, that effect was given to decisions taken by the Governor in the Council of Ministers relating to such matters. This was one of the potential sources of friction between the Centre and the Regions.

. . . . .

Sir Arthur Richards in his address to the first meeting of the legislature under the Richards Constitution described the administrative service as 'the scaffolding which supports those working on a new building in process of erection until the building is ready to stand alone and the scaffolding can be removed'. He warned that if the administrative scaffolding was removed prematurely from the new building the building would be incomplete and might collapse. The framers of the 1951 Constitution took this injunction seriously to heart. Therefore, despite the wide measure of legislative and executive authority conferred upon the Regions, the public service remained unified. The old power structure between the Governor and Lieutenant-Governors, and between the heads of Central Government departments and Regional Directors, remained unchanged. Power to appoint (including power to promote or transfer) and power to dismiss and to exercise disciplinary control over public officers were all vested in the Governor. The Governor, with the consent of the Secretary of State for the Colonies, could delegate certain of these powers to the Lieutenant-Governors, but the ultimate responsibility devolved on him. He was advised by a Public Service Commission, but he was not obliged to act in accordance with the advice of the Commission.

The delegates to the General Conference on the Nigerian Constitution could not in January 1950 have foreseen that their anxiety to maintain the unity of the country would result in such a complicated and rigid constitutional arrangement; nor did the legal draftsmen who interpreted what they believed to be the decisions of the General Conference envisage the dynamic development of political parties. The general belief in Nigeria at that time was that no single political party could command sufficient popular support throughout the country to enable it to win a majority of the seats in the House of Representatives. Most Nigerians accepted the new constitution as a challenge which demanded that the best men the country could provide should come forward to serve it. But political parties did develop, and limited as the opportunities were for electioneering under the new dispensation, the parties conducted vigorous campaigns for control of the legislatures.

The parties (the N.C.N.C. excepted) concentrated their efforts on controlling the Regional legislatures: the N.P.C., the Northern; the Action Group, the Western; and the N.C.N.C. (grudgingly) the Eastern. The immediate result of this was that the majority party in each Regional legislature not only provided all the Regional Ministers in the Executive Council, but nominated the four Central Ministers from the Region and provided the overwhelming majority of the members of the House of Representatives from that Region. Therefore, in both the House of Representatives from each Region and in the Council of Ministers, members were expected by their party to act as delegates from their respective Regions. At the Regional level, the operation of the party system under a constitution which made no provision for it created stresses almost from the start. For instance, Section 135 of the Order-in-Council provided for the order of precedence among members of the Executive Council: after the Lieutenant-Governor, *ex-officio* and official members, came Regional Ministers according to the length of time that they had served continuously in their posts. The constitution made no provision for appointing a Leader of Government Business. However, when the Action Group, the majority party in the Western Region, took office in January 1952, it insisted that the leader of the party be recognized by the Lieutenant-Governor as Leader of Government Business and be accorded precedence over the other Ministers.

In the Eastern Region a far more serious situation arose early in 1953. The Regional Ministers who were all members of the majority party, the N.C.N.C., fell foul of their party leaders and were induced at an all-night meeting to sign printed letters of resignation in accordance with Section 131(2) of the Constitution. However, before the letters of resignation were received by the Lieutenant-Governor, each of the Ministers submitted a letter to the Lieutenant-Governor countermanding his 'letter of resignation', claiming that he had signed it under duress, and declaring, therefore, that he wanted it disregarded. On the advice of the Law Officers of the Region, the Lieutenant-Governor decided that each of the Ministers had not, 'by writing under his hand addressed to the Lieutenant-Governor', resigned his seat in the Executive Council of the Region as laid down by Section 131 (2) of the Constitution; he, therefore, exercised his discretionary power under Section 134 of the Constitution to decide that each of the Regional Ministers had a right to remain a member of the Regional Executive Council.[23] This decision precipitated an immediate constitutional crisis, and some members of the N.C.N.C. challenged the Lieutenant-Governor's decision by filing a writ of *Quo Warranto* in the High Court against each of the Ministers, demanding that he should show by what authority he continued to perform the functions of a Regional Minister; but the applications were all struck out by the Court for want of prosecution by the applicants. Infuriated by their inability to remove the Regional Ministers through the normal constitutional methods, the leaders of the N.C.N.C. resorted to different ones. In the House of Assembly itself they exploited the provisions of the Standing Orders to paralyse the business of the House for weeks on end and block the passage of the annual Appropriation Bill. Outside the House they encouraged their supporters to harass the Ministers and create such an atmosphere of tension that a dissolution of the legislature appeared to be the only solution to the crisis.

A few weeks after the Eastern Region crisis, the 'Macpherson' Constitution was shaken to its very foundation. The split inside the ranks of the N.C.N.C. had provided the Action Group with an opportunity to stake its claim for national leadership and to establish itself as a popular party. Accordingly at the Budget Meeting of the House of Representatives in March 1953, the Action Group sponsored a Private Member's Motion calling upon the House to accept 'as a primary political objective the attainment of self-government for Nigeria in 1956'. The Northern Members of the House were sure that the motion was directed against them. They believed that it was designed to bring Northern leaders into public contempt as stooges of the British civil servants, since they could not in all conscience support a motion for self-government within three years from 1953. The Council of Ministers spent many anxious hours trying to find a way out of the dilemma. It was clear that if the House debated the motion and took a vote, the division would be on Regional lines. The West and the East would support the motion and the North would oppose it, with an inevitable embitterment of relations between the North and the South. A majority of the Council of Ministers thought that if the Action Group persisted in debating the motion, then the government should abstain from voting in order to avoid a split in the Cabinet. Within the twelve months since the Council of Ministers had been established, mutual confidence had been slowly nourished, and it was in the interest of the country that no public action of the government or legislature should be permitted to destroy that confidence. Accordingly, behind-the-scene efforts were made to postpone the debate and allow time for consultation. But all these failed, and the debate took place on 31 March 1953.

Chief Anthony Enahoro, who moved the motion, made a brilliant and most persuasive speech in support of the necessity for the House publicly to declare its support for the objective of self-government in 1956, but he left no one in any doubt of his intention to embarrass all those who held such timing to be inappropriate when he mildly threatened that the vote at the end of the debate would reveal who were the 'true nationalists'. For the N.C.N.C. this was an opportunity publicly to pillory the Eastern members of the Council of Ministers, whom the N.C.N.C. had just then expelled from their party for writing an 'uncomplimentary' letter to its President.

The implications of these words were not lost on the Northern leaders; and when the Sardauna of Sokoto rose to move an amendment to the substantive motion, substituting the words 'as soon as practicable' for '1956' he left no one in any doubt that he thought Chief Enahoro's 'true nationalists' were the Southern politicians. He believed that the original motion was deliberately designed to destroy the inter-Regional relationship which the Constitution was rapidly building up and to cause ill-feeling between the North and the South. He declared that some Southern Nigerians and their newspapers had for many years led the outside world to regard Northern Nigeria as a backward area, where all the people were conservative – and unreceptive to modern ideas. On the contrary, he said, the North was working hard towards self-government, but would not be stampeded into taking precipitate action. However, the North would not obstruct any Region which wanted self-government in 1956.

Another member of the Northern People's Congress then successfully moved a dilatory motion under the Standing Orders of the House, in order to end the debate without taking a vote on either the amendment or the substantive motion.[24] The Action Group and the N.C.N.C. decided that they could no longer put up with the attempt to postpone a vote on the substantive motion and so walked out of the House. Predictably, when the Northern members left the House at the end of the next day's sitting, a crowd, provoked by the politicians, booed and jeered the Northerners, calling them 'imperialist stooges'; and but for the intervention of the police, the legislators would have been severely mauled. Both the N.C.N.C. and the Action Group geared up their party machines and newspapers for a country-wide campaign to discredit the Northern legislators (as well as those Eastern legislators who had not joined in the walk-out following the frustration of the self-government motion) as traitors and agents of the British imperialists. For their part the Northerners, helped by the attacks of the Southern press against Northern Emirs and political leaders, had no difficulty in firing anti-Southern feeling in Northern townships; and within six weeks of the Lagos incident a violent communal explosion occurred in the cosmopolitan city of Kano, resulting in the loss of at least thirty-six lives and considerable damage to property. For four days (from 16 to 19 May) Southerners and Northerners in this bustling commercial capital of the Northern Region were attacking each other, burning and pillaging each other's property, mutilating the bodies of victims, and committing the most violent atrocities on one another in the mass hysteria which gripped the town. It took the combined efforts of the Administration, police and army to restore peace.[25]

On 21 May 1953, the Secretary of State for the Colonies announced in the House of Commons that:

> Her Majesty's Government has regretfully decided that the Nigerian Constitution will have to be redrawn to provide for greater Regional autonomy and for the removal of powers of intervention by the Centre in matters which could, without detriment to other Regions, be placed entirely within Regional competence. It will be necessary to ensure that the common economic and defence requirements of all Regions are secured and, in order to guarantee this and at the same time to preserve the common interests of all the peoples of the territory, there will be a continuing need for a Central Organization. The work of redrawing the Constitution, having regard to the complicated problems involved, will inevitably take time. Her Majesty's Government will, however, wish to cooperate in this process as closely as possible with the leaders of the peoples in all

three Regions, and as a first step proposes to invite representatives from each Region to London for discussions.

This was a great victory for the regionalists, but significantly there was no reference to the issue of self-government for Nigeria at all.

The conference of representatives assembled in London throughout July and August and, after protracted debates and argument, decided:

(i) that the Regional Governments should in the sphere of activities assigned to them be more independent of the Central Government, and hence that Regional legislation should not have to be submitted to the Central Executive;
(ii) that residual functions should be vested in the Regional Governments, and a limited number of subjects allocated exclusively to the Federal authority;
(iii) that membership of the House of Representatives should be enlarged to 184 elected members and 3 *ex-officio* members (the Chief Secretary to the Government, the Financial Secretary, and the Attorney-General); that in elections to the Regional legislatures, there need be no uniformity in electoral procedure between Regions; that new Provincial Electoral Colleges should be established to elect Northern members to the Federal legislature; and that in the Eastern and Western Regions, arrangements should be made to permit separate elections to the Centre on a divisional basis;
(iv) that the Council of Ministers should consist of 9 elected members (three from each Region) and the 3 *ex-officio* members who would be members of the legislature.

The Conference decided that there was no need to insist on uniformity in the structure of the Regional Governments, and so the majority delegation from each Region (the N.P.C. for the North, N.C.N.C. for the East, and the Action Group for the West) submitted proposals for its own Region. The main features of the Regional proposals were that the existing Regional legislatures should be expanded and their *ex-officio* membership reduced; the office of Premier was created, and the number of elected members in the Regional Executive Councils was increased.

On the issue of self-government, the Secretary of State for the Colonies told the Conference that Britain was not prepared to fix a definite date for Nigeria as a whole, the more so as the Northern delegation, representing over half the population of Nigeria, was unable to depart from its policy of self-government as soon as practicable. The Conference, however, accepted a declaration of policy that in 1956 the British Government would grant to those Regions which so desired it 'self-government' in respect of all matters within the competence of the Regional Government, which in practice meant that they could deal direct with the Colonial Office in those matters.

The new constitutional arrangements which emerged from the decisions of this Conference came into effect on 1 October 1954, and though they retained the structural framework of three Regions provided for in the 1951 Constitution, radical changes were introduced. Nigeria became a Federation of three Regions each of which exercised full legislative and executive authority within its area of jurisdiction, except for the reservation to the Federal Government of exclusive powers over a number of subjects, set out in the 'Exclusive Subjects List', and including railways, harbours, shipping, civil aviation, postal and telecommunication services, mining, external and inter-Regional trade, customs, banking, currency and exchange control, external relations, immigration and emigration, citizenship and defence. On certain other subjects, set out in a second list called the 'Concurrent List', both the Regional and Federal authorities exercised concurrent jurisdiction; but subject to the express proviso in the Constitution that in the event of any conflict between a Regional law and a Federal law over a matter on the Concurrent List, the Federal law should prevail.

Lagos was again separated from the Western Region and designated Federal territory, with the right to elect two representatives to the House of Representatives; and the Trust Territory of the Southern Cameroons, hitherto administered as part of the Eastern Region, became a quasi-Federal territory, having its own legislature and Executive Council, but no ministerial responsibility.

The Regional legislatures no longer acted as electoral colleges, and separate and direct elections were held to the House of Representatives.

In place of a unified civil service, four public services were created, one for each Region and one for the Federation. The judiciary too was regionalized. A High Court was established for each Region, and one for Lagos and the Cameroons; and a Federal Supreme Court was created to exercise the appellate jurisdiction of the former West African Court of Appeal, as well as original jurisdiction in disputes between the Regional Governments or between any Regional Government and the Federal Government. Finally, the four Produce Marketing Boards which had hitherto dealt with the principal produce – cocoa, palm oil and kernels, groundnuts, cotton – on a national basis, were replaced by four all-purposes Regional Marketing Boards, and a Central Marketing Board which acted as an agent for the Regional Boards in handling the shipment and overseas sales of produce purchased by the Regional Boards.

The 1954 Constitution was the kernel of all further constitutional changes, which culminated in the establishment of the Federal Republic of Nigeria on 1 October 1963. But during the intervening years several amendments were made, some of which intensified the strains which existed between the different communities in the country. For instance, on the regionalization of the Nigerian civil service and the creation of four separate public services, each Regional Government recalled the ablest of the Nigerian public servants from Lagos and other Regions to their Region of origin, where they were in most cases placed in important policy-forming posts above public servants from other Regions. This produced discontent in the public services and, worse still, it denuded the federal service of experienced Nigerians who should at that time have been preparing themselves to take over the burden of running the public service of an independent Nigeria. At the political level, each of the leaders of the major political parties retired to his Region of origin to become the Regional Premier, while his lieutenants were sent to participate in the Federal Government, and this inevitably tended to make the Federal Government (with its overwhelming expatriate staff) function as an agent of the Regional Governments.

In 1957, the Eastern and Western Regions became self-governing in matters within their competence. This meant that the Regional Premier, instead of the Governor, presided over meetings of the Executive Council, and that the Regional legislature could debate any motion and pass any law without hindrance by the Governor, except where the law was inconsistent with any treaty obligation, or was likely to prejudice the Royal Prerogative, trade, transport or communications in any part of the Commonwealth, the property rights of British subjects not residing in Nigeria, or the continuance of federal government.

Because the majority party in each Region drew most of its support in the legislature from members of one linguistic group, and the bulk of the opposition was drawn from outside that linguistic group, there were widespread fears amongst minority groups in the Regions that self-government would facilitate their political and economic subjugation to the interests of the majorities. These fears gave birth to widespread demands for the creation of new states out of the existing three Regions – demands which vindicated the stand taken by the Nigeria Society at the General Conference in 1950 – and the problem of how to protect minority rights in an independent Nigeria was, therefore, one of the most important items on the agenda of the Nigerian Constitutional Conferences held in London in 1957 and 1958. At the 1957 Conference, the Secretary of State for the Colonies was requested to appoint a Commission that would examine the fears of minorities in any part of Nigeria and propose means of allaying them. The Minorities Commission (as it was named) found as a fact that many of the fears expressed by minorities were genuine, but did not think that these fears could be removed by splitting the three Regions of Nigeria into yet smaller Regions. Instead, the Commission placed at the forefront of its recommendations for protecting minorities a provision in the Constitution of a comprehensive list of 'Fundamental Human Rights' and the maintenance of a single police force for the country under Federal Government control, with arrangements to enable the Regional Governments to participate in the management of the force.* The Commission also made a number of minor recommendations, such as the establishment of Minority Areas and Special Areas, not only to allay fears, but to facilitate social and economic progress amongst the minority groups.

* For more detailed study of the Commission's assessment and recommendations see ch. 6., pp. 96–103.

By 1957, no difference existed over the timing of independence among the major parties, each of them being now firmly in control of the Region which it represented. Indeed, at the 1957 Conference, the three Regional leaders presented a joint memorandum demanding self-government for Nigeria in 1959. Therefore, apart from the minorities issue, the two post-independence Conferences were devoted to making the 1954 Constitution suitable for an independent country, by settling such final provisions as the division of functions between the Federal and self-governing Regional Governments, electoral arrangements, fundamental rights, national security, Nigerian citizenship and the representation of Nigeria overseas. The decisions of these Conferences were ultimately embodied in the Nigeria (Constitution) Order-in-Council, 1960, which constituted the Schedule to the Nigeria Independence Act passed by the United Kingdom Parliament in that year. And so, on 1 October 1960, Nigeria came to the end of the journey begun by the Oba Dosunmy of Lagos nearly one hundred years before. As a sovereign independent country, she was admitted to United Nations membership, and within a week of attaining this status was called upon to help in policing the strife-torn Congo Republic. But Nigeria's struggle to become a nation in fact as well as in legal theory had hardly begun.

On 16 November 1960, the last British Governor-General gave way to a Nigerian, Dr Nnamdi Azikiwe, himself one of the foremost architects of independence, and three years later, on 1 October 1963, Nigeria became a republic within the Commonwealth. These external and visible signs of the country's determination to assert its claim to nationhood did not, however, diminish the genuine anxiety of many Nigerians and some overseas friends of Nigeria that in a real and organic sense Nigeria was still some distance from the goal of one nation; and many put the blame on the federal system of government.

6. The Problems of Federalism in Nigeria

Constitutions are not ends in themselves but means by which human communities order their affairs and direct their efforts towards self-perpetuation. But men, not documents, make written constitutions work. The best constitution will fail to produce the greatest good for the greatest number if the men who work it lack the ability to settle their differences, the courage to admit mistakes, and above all the determination to place the interest of the community above that of the constituent individual or group. This is especially true of federal constitutions, the basis of which is compromise. For these reasons Nigerian political leaders spent the last seven years before independence in trying to find a constitutional arrangement satisfactory to them all.

Many Federations come into existence by agreement among a number of hitherto separate and independent authorities which decide to transfer some functions and services to a newly created general government. In such cases there is as a rule relatively little difficulty in deciding the limits of the new federal authority. The Federation of Nigeria came into existence by the reverse process: a formerly unitary government surrendered powers and functions to newly created Regional authorities. It is incorrect to suppose that the Federal Constitution of 1954 merely re-established a structural arrangement which existed prior to 1947. There was never a time in Nigerian history when the Northern, Eastern or Western Regions existed as distinct political entities; although they incorporated old kingdoms and emirates within their areas of jurisdiction, they came into existence in comparatively recent times only as a result of deliberate political and administrative action.

Nigeria moved from unitary to federal government and in the process created numerical majorities on the one hand and minorities on the other.[26] This fact was to reveal itself as of the utmost significance for the future of Nigerian federalism. Like India (and, in small measure, Canada), Nigeria is beset with the problem of plural cultures and a multiplicity of languages. Nigerian federalism was, therefore, deeply rooted in social diversity; and the framers of the Constitution were preoccupied by the extent to which diversity should be recognized in the Constitution without doing violence to the concept of one Nigeria. They responded by investing the Regional Governments with residual powers over a wide range of subjects which affected most directly the everyday life of the people, like local government, land use, education and health. It is interesting to note that, faced with a similar issue, the delegates who assembled in 1867 to redraw the Canadian Constitution were convinced that a tight federation with an extensive measure of provincial autonomy was the way out of a defective union in which the proper enjoyment of self-government was hampered by cultural and linguistic discords, and while recognizing the cultural diversity of the community, also recognized the need for a strong central government in order to build up national prestige and power, to establish stable institutions of credit, to stimulate the flow of capital from abroad, and to increase industrial potential. The Dominion Government was, therefore, invested with residual powers.* This has progressively strengthened the Canadian Government at the expense of the Provincial Governments. In Australia, whose constitutional provisions Nigeria in larger measure adopted, the States started their political career as separate entities but later came under one general government through the passing by the United Kingdom Parliament of the Commonwealth of Australia Act. Unlike the Regions of Nigeria, the Australian States contain people of the same cultural and linguistic group. Federalism in Australia, is, therefore, less deeply rooted in social diversity and is free from the difficulties which usually arise from the existence of plural cultures, a multiplicity of languages and significant racial minorities; besides, Australia was not threatened by the same imperial pressures from a neighbour as Canada was from the United States of America. Therefore, the delegates from the

* i.e. powers in all fields but certain specified ones of 'local' concern.

various Australian States who gathered at the different constitutional conventions between 1890 and 1898 did not feel the same protective urge for centralism as did the Canadian delegates in 1867. The result was that the Australians rejected the Canadian distribution of legislative powers between federal and regional authorities in favour of the American pattern which vests residual powers in the regional legislatures. However, because of the basically favourable social environment which exists in Australia, the absence of dual cultures, the racial homogeneity and the unifying influence of the English language, the Australian State Governments and Federal Government, though distinct and coordinate, often pursue similar paths in their social and economic policies. Indeed, the modern trend towards closer co-operation between Federal and State Governments has not only furthered centralism in Australia but has facilitated the acceptance by the States of the pre-eminence of the Federal Government in the Australian union. Indeed, Australia, with a loose federal structure, practises something closely akin to unitary government. Nigeria, without the same homogeneous cultural environment as Australia, chose the Australian pattern of government, with all the implications and problems of a loose federation.

Political and Administrative Problems

The main political argument for adopting a federal system in Nigeria was that the size of the country and its ethnic and cultural diversity militated against the successful operation of a unitary government. If, it was claimed, the unitary administrative structure of Nigeria were broken down into a federal system, power would be dispersed, regional autonomy secured for each cultural group (Hausa, Ibo and Yoruba), and each group would thereby be enabled to develop at its own pace and in accordance with its natural resources and capabilities. The framers of the constitution, therefore, went the whole way in adopting an Australian-type federal structure with its rigid limitations on the right of the federal authority to encroach upon the powers of the Regions. But the new Nigerian Federation lacked two of the main factors which that eminent authority on federalism K. C. Wheare, in his study of 'Some Pre-Requisities of Federal Government'[27], considers essential to successful federal government: (1) economic divergence of interest between the units, but without any one unit having an overwhelming preponderance in population or resources; and (2) 'a previous existence of the federating states as distinct colonies or states with governments of their own'. Nor, in the case of Nigeria, were the federating states culturally homogeneous. On the contrary each of the three Regions, as they existed at the time of federation in 1954, consisted of a majority cultural group of about two-thirds of the population, and one or more minority groups amounting to about one-third.

These minorities, as we have seen, became apprehensive at the adoption of a loose federation for the country and demanded the establishment of separate states as a means of protecting their interests. The Commission appointed to advise on measures for allaying minority fears, taking a purely legalistic attitude in its examination of the claims for new states, rejected the idea of re-dividing the three Regions into smaller administrative units on a linguistic or cultural basis. Of the number of constitutional safe-guards it proposed instead, some were embodied in the 1958 and retained in the present Constitution – most importantly, Federal control of the Nigeria police and the inclusion of a chapter on Fundamental Rights in the Constitution. The Minorities Commission was satisfied on the evidence before it that, in addition to some denial of social amenities, minorities in every Region suffered physical molestation from 'strong-arm groups' supporting the party in power and ready to intimidate and coerce political opponents. The Commission believed, without any evidence, that no government which sought to continue in office indefinitely could long neglect the provision of amenities to any constituency. But with a majority assured by the solid core of the Regional constituencies, no Regional Government needed to worry very much about the views of the minority. As regards physical molestation, the Commission believed that the fears of minorities could best be allayed by the creation of a centrally controlled police force which would be free of political party control. It urged that the appointment of the Inspector-General of the Nigeria Police and of the Regional Commissioners of Police should be strictly safeguarded by special constitutional provisions; and that the training and equipment of all police forces should be coordinated by a federal police organisation.

Sections 98 to 103 of the Nigeria Constitution accordingly provided that:

> The Nigeria Police shall be under the command of the Inspector-General of the Nigeria Police, and any contingents of the Nigeria Police Force stationed in a Region shall, subject to the authority of the Inspector-General of the Nigeria Police, be under the command of the Commissioner of Police of that Region. The Prime Minister may give to the Inspector-General of the Nigeria Police such directions with respect to the maintaining and securing of public safety and public order as he may consider necessary, and the Inspector-General shall comply with those directions or cause them to be complied with.
>
> The Commissioner of Police of a Region shall comply with the directions of the Premier of a Region with respect to the maintaining and securing of public safety and public order within the Region or cause them to be complied with: Provided that before carrying out any such directions, the Commissioner may request that the matter should be referred to the Prime Minister for his directions.

The Constitution also provided for the establishment of a Nigeria Police Council, with power to supervise the organization and administration of the Nigeria Police; and a Police Service Commission with responsibility for the appointment, promotion, dismissal and discipline of members of the Nigeria Police.

From the start of independence, the Nigeria police constituted the first line of defence in the battle to maintain law and order, and the stability and internal security of the country. During periods of civil commotion or emergency, they discharged their responsibilities with commendable efficiency. But it cannot justly be claimed that they were always effective in protecting minority groups, whether ethnic or political, against physical molestation, discrimination or victimization by the corresponding majority groups. Police action was based on clearly defined legal principles. The police could protect individuals or groups against assault from other more powerful individuals or groups. They could not defend them against discrimination or victimization which were not offences under Nigerian law.

The top ranks of the police hierarchy displayed in general a high sense of duty and impartiality. But these attributes did not percolate very far down the rank-and-file of the force. Many a junior policeman on beat sometimes allowed his tribal prejudices or political persuasion to colour his vision in critical situations. And the control of police forces was rendered even more irrelevant to the minority problem by the existence of Local Government Police establishments which were subjected to even greater political pressures in the Regions than was the Nigeria Police. Indeed, most complaints at election time were directed against the Local Government Police forces, who were less trained and less disciplined than the Nigeria Police, and readily succumbed to the pressure of a majority party to act as its agents.

The second constitutional safeguard lay in the provisions of Fundamental Rights. Chapter III of the Constitution was a Bill of Rights based on the European Convention on Human Rights. It included the right to life; the right to protection against inhuman treatment, slavery or servitude; the right to liberty and the right to a fair determination of the individual's civil and criminal rights; the right to private life, freedom of conscience, freedom of expression, freedom of assembly and freedom of movement; the right to protection against discrimination on grounds of tribe or religion; and the right to protection against the appropriation of property.

The Constitution also made extensive provisions for the enforcement of these rights by the Courts; any person who alleged that his fundamental rights had been contravened could apply for redress to the High Court of the Region in which he resided, and the High Court could make any order, issue any writs, or give any directions as it saw fit for the purpose of enforcing the rights. There was also a right of appeal from all decisions of the High Court to the Supreme Court of Nigeria.

The purpose of the Bill of Rights was avowedly the protection of minorities. It could, therefore, properly be contended that although the Court was bound to give the fullest consideration to the views of the majority of the legislators when interpreting a right, it should be guided by the standard of reasonableness in societies other than Nigeria. But to adopt such canons of interpretation placed on the Courts the responsibility for choosing between different political, economic and social policies, a responsibility which created the risk of conflict between the Courts and the legislature; and on the few occasions when the Courts were called upon to pronounce on issues of fundamental rights, they declared without the slightest hesitation that their yardstick of 'what is reasonably justifiable in a democratic society' must be limited to reasonableness under Nigerian conditions. Furthermore, the Courts confirmed that the constitutional provisions on fundamental rights did not override the statute law of Nigeria. For example, Sections 33, 34 and 35 of the Children's and Young Persons' Law, 1958, of Northern Nigeria prohibited persons under the age of sixteen years from engaging in political activities. When these provisions were challenged in the High Court of Northern Nigeria on the ground that they contravened the constitutional rights to 'freedom of expression', peaceful assembly and association, and freedom of conscience, the Court held that though these provisions of the Regional law did indeed infringe fundamental rights, the Regional law was 'reasonably justifiable in the democratic society of Northern Nigeria', on the grounds that the legislature deemed such legislation necessary in the interest of public morals and public order. What was 'democratic', therefore, depended upon the political circumstances at any given time and place.

In another case, a person held in custody on a charge of treasonable felony was refused the right to retain the services of a foreign Counsel resident outside the country. He challenged the Order of the Federal Minister of Internal Affairs prohibiting the entry into Nigeria of the non-Nigerian lawyer; but the Lagos High Court ruled that, although Section 22(5) (*c*) of the Constitution gave to any person charged with a criminal offence the right 'to defend himself in person or by legal representatives of his own choice', the Section did not derogate from the Minister's right under Section 13 of the Immigration Act to prohibit, in his absolute discretion, the entry into Nigeria of any person not a native of Nigeria.

The constitutional provisions for the protection of fundamental rights did not, accordingly, prevent the unobtrusive encroachment of governments and their agencies on the rights of individuals. And their value as a safeguard for minority interests proved to be even less, especially in the most vital spheres of economic and social discrimination, discrimination in appointments to public service posts, and political coercion. In any region where the government party had an assured majority through the support of one main interest-group, it was difficult for the government of that Region not to put the interests of the majority group before that of minorities.

Section 27(1) of the Constitution prohibited discrimination against citizens of Nigeria on the grounds of tribe, place of origin, religion or political opinion. Yet some governments officially espoused the policy of discrimination against Nigerians from other Regions or tribes in their recruitment policies, as a means of ensuring employment opportunities for the indigenes of their Regions – a policy which, needless to say, yielded large electoral dividends. Furthermore, Section 27(2) (*d*) of the Constitution exempted from the operation of Section 27(1) any law which 'imposes any disability or accords any privilege or advantage that, having regard to its nature and to special circumstances pertaining to the persons to whom it applies, is reasonably justifiable in a democratic society'. A government which legislated against the admission to its public service of persons from other Regions could, if challenged, fall back on the escape clause provided by Section 27(2).

One of the strongest fears repeatedly raised before the Minorities Commission related to the expropriation of the communal lands of minority groups by persons of the majority group with government support. Being unfamiliar with the social value of land in African communities, the Commission showed no sympathy with such fears, and came out rather forcefully, if unintentionally, in support of the land speculators who in the name of economic development got government agreement to take land from the minority communities. The Minorities Commission recommended that legislation ought to be introduced to regulate the acquisition of land; and Section 30 of Chapter III of the Federal Constitution was designed to ensure that any person whose property was the subject of compulsory acquisition should be compensated. But this provision protected members of the majority groups as much as those of the minority groups. It did not deal with the economic dilemmas which ethnic minorities in a federal system had to face. Any government which depends for its survival on one interest-group tends to cater more for the economic interests of that group than for those of other groups; thus, in the allocation of building sites in a developing urban community, for example, the interests of members of the majority group tend to take precedence over those of others within the same community, exacerbating tribal divisions and eroding national unity.

The framers of the Constitution recognized that, in spite of constitutional safeguards, there might be intangible reasons, such as ethnic or language pride, promoting demands for a separate political organization within the federal union. Section 4 of the Constitution, therefore, made elaborate provisions for altering the existing Regional boundaries in order to create new Regions. A proposal for the creation of a new Region out of an existing one had to be submitted to each House of Parliament and, if the proposal was approved by a resolution of each of the Houses, and supported by the votes of at least two-thirds of all the members of that House, it had then to be submitted to the legislative houses of all the Regions. It had to be approved by a simple majority of the members of each Regional legislature: or by the legislatures of at least two Regional Houses, including the legislature of the Region from which the new Region was to be carved. Parliament had then to enact a law providing for such constitutional amendments as were necessary to give effect to the proposal and this law was then to be submitted for approval by resolution of each of the legislative houses of at least two Regions. The Federal Electoral Commission was then to hold a referendum in the area which it was proposed to convert into a new Region. All persons who were entitled to vote at elections to the House of Representatives might vote at the referendum, and at least sixty per cent of those who in fact voted had to be in favour of the proposal for a new Region before the Act creating it could come into effect.

This extremely cumbersome and rigid procedure was supposedly to discourage frivolous demands for new states and to check fissiparous tendencies among Nigerian communities. The events of the Western Nigeria crisis in 1962, however, clearly demonstrated that rigid though the constitutional machinery might be, new Regions could be created by the fiat of the majority ethnic groups. A combination of the North and the East (Fulani-Hausa and Ibo) succeeded in depriving the Yoruba of Western Nigeria of their satellites, the Bini, Western Ibo, Itshekeri and Urhobo, to constitute the new Mid-West Region. The constitutional machinery was set in motion and carried through parliament and the Regional legislatures in the proper democratic way, but there was not the slightest doubt that the Mid-West state was created not solely to allay the fears of the minorities in that area but to neutralize Action Group influence there. The same people who opposed the creation of the Mid-West state in 1957 unanimously supported it in 1962.

Thus, while the constitutional proposal for creating new states was supposed to be the ultimate safeguard for protecting minorities, in practice it increased the political dominance of majority interests over those of the minorities. Every minority group is obliged by the logic of events to identify itself with the interests of one or other of the majority groups. Identification with the right majority will yield political advantages, and vice versa. This is at least in part the reason why Nigerian legislatures abounded with opportunists who believed that their personal interests were better served by selling out to the majority party than by remaining loyal to the minority opposition group. The irony was that, with the exception of the North which maintained a solid Fulani–Hausa front, the majority ethnic group in every Region might find itself in the position of a minority on any issue according to the political alignments of the parties in the federation at a particular time, rendering consistency in public policy difficult to maintain. The minority problem, more than any other single political issue, was at the root of most of the friction between and within political parties, governments and administration since Independence.

On the eve of the 1957 Constitutional Conference, the then Regional Premiers, the Sarduana of Sokoto, Dr Nnamdi Azikiwe and Chief Obafemi Awolowo, met to review the agitation of minority elements for the creation of separate states. The Premiers appeared to have given serious consideration to the proposals for new states, and in a draft statement which they distributed to Nigerian delegates before the conference assembled, they set out the principles upon which any proposal for the creation of new Regions out of the existing three Regions should be based. Indeed at some of the pre-conference meetings, the three major political parties appeared willing to submit a joint memorandum on the creation of states which would embody four principles: (1) the desire for self-determination; (2) cultural relationship; (3) geographical propinquity; and (4) economic viability.

The draft memorandum put before delegates from the minority areas at the pre-conference meeting in May 1957, read as follows:

> The Premiers and their advisers were agreed that new states should be created and based on the following principles:
> (*a*) the wishes of the people of the area should be determined by plebiscite;
> (*b*) the creation of new States should be consistent with the principles of viability;
> (*c*) the component units of the new States should be geographically contiguous;
> (*d*) no ethnic group should be split into new States except with the express wishes of a two-third majority of the people in the ethnic group, determined by plebiscite.[28]

On the strength of the assurances based on this draft memorandum, delegates from the minority groups, constituting one-third of the Nigerian delegation to the Conference, agreed not to hamper the negotiations for independence which the Premiers were conducting with the Colonial Office. That the draft memorandum never reached the Conference table was an illustration of the tendency to place expediency before principle so characteristic of Nigerian politics to the detriment of national unity and stability. The bitterness which followed the hastily prepared and unnecessarily dogmatic report of the Minorities Commission is now history. Individual Nigerian politicians might make their peace with the majority parties, whole groups of minority communities might be cowed into mass support for the majority governing parties and be thankful for the 'small mercies' which they received. Yet their frustration and resentment against the existing order remained deep. Such does not make for peace and stability. The Western Nigeria emergency and the creation of the Mid-West Region underscored the falsity of most of the assumptions upon which the Minorities Commission's recommendations were based. They inexorably pointed to the conclusion that the existing political structure of the Federation would not endure for long.

Economic and Fiscal Problems

The division of political and fiscal powers between the new Federal Government and the Regional Governments reflected the desire of the majority interests represented at the constitutional conference of 1953 to reduce the Central Government to a mere agency of the Regional Governments. The Conference agreed to the appointment of a Fiscal Commissioner to advise on the allocation of revenue between the Federal Government and the Regional Governments, but his terms of reference were narrowly circumscribed. He was, among other things, enjoined:

> to assess the net cost of the central services and the services remaining to be undertaken by the Regions; and, in the light of the above, to inquire how the revenues available, or to be made available to the Regions and to the Centre can best be collected and distributed, having regard on the one hand to the need to provide to the Regions and the Centre an adequate measure of fiscal autonomy within their own sphere of government and, on the other, to the importance of ensuring that the total revenues available to Nigeria are allocated in such a way that the principle of derivation is followed to the fullest degree compatible with meeting the reasonable needs of the Centre and each of the Regions.

This restricted brief was the culmination of a prolonged dispute over the equity of the territorial distribution of public revenues and social amenities by the Central Government in past years. In 1946 a report was prepared for the Central Government by Sir Sydney Phillipson, under the title, 'Financial and Administrative Procedure under the New Constitution'.[29] One of the objects of that (the Richards) Constitution was to forge political and constitutional links between the Native Authorities and the Legislative Council. Regional Assemblies were created, but they had no legislative authority, and no legal power of appropriating revenue for Regional expenditure. All revenues available for Regional purposes, whatever their source, were noted by the Legislative Council of Nigeria as lump sum grants, with each grant constituting a separate head of expenditure in the Estimates of Nigeria. And so the Phillipson Report dealt with (*a*) what items of revenue other than the Regional share of direct taxation should be declared Regional, and (*b*) the basis of allocation to the Regions of non-

Regional revenues. All revenues identifiable with the Region and locally collected by the Regional authorities were declared Regional. All other revenues were non-Regional. Phillipson had then to devise a formula for the division of the non-Regional revenue between the Central Government and the new Regional administrations. He considered in turn the principle of derivation, under which each Region's share of the central revenue would be proportionate to its contribution to that revenue derived from customs duties and company tax, and the principle of need, on the basis of which each Region would receive according to its needs, with population suggested as the best measure. The Western and Northern Regional authorities favoured the principle of derivation (although the North preferred a combination of derivation and need). The East stood for the principle of need alone. On the basis of derivation, the principle finally recommended by Phillipson, the North was at that time contributing far more than it was receiving, and the Eastern Region was receiving appreciably higher revenue than it was contributing. The West also contributed rather more than it received. The period under consideration, it must be remembered, was one of high export prices for tin, groundnuts, and cocoa, all primary commodities produced by the North and West. Palm oil, the chief export of the East, had not completely recovered from the slump.

The Nigerian Government, while accepting the principle of derivation, decided that in the national interest the situation required progressive adjustment until the relative levels of Regional expenditure should be brought into correspondence with the relative contributions of the Regions to the total central revenues of Nigeria. This decision was embodied in the Statement of Administrative and Financial Procedure in the following terms:

(i) The interests of Nigeria as a whole must always determine the allocation of revenues and other public funds for Nigerian and Regional expenditure.

(ii) Subject to the fundamental principle stated in sub-paragraph (i) above and also to the condition that more should not be allocated than can reasonably be expended, it will be an objective of policy to achieve, as early as may be and in any event within a period of five years, a condition of things in which it will be possible to allocate to each Region for expenditure on Regional services and works:

(*a*) the full amount of the government share of tax collected under the Direct Taxation Ordinance (as subsequently amended) and all other revenues declared Regional;

(*b*) a grant from the other revenues of Nigeria not included in (*a*) or from the other public funds of Nigeria, in strict proportion to the contribution which the Region makes to those other revenues.

This decision was reluctantly accepted by the North and the West, who were convinced that the East, with its larger primary school enrolment and intricate network of roads (most of them provided by communal labour), was being subsidized by the other Regions. At meetings of the legislature and during the Constitutional Conference of 1950 there was much inter-Regional misunderstanding and friction over the sharing of revenue, all of which had unhappy consequences in both political and administrative spheres, and coloured the views reflected in the terms of reference laid down for the new Hicks–Phillipson Revenue Allocation Commission.

Commenting on that section in its terms of reference which directed that 'if investigation by the expert Commission proves that one Region had been unfairly treated during past years, that Region should be allowed a block grant so as to make up for part of what it has lost', the Hicks–Phillipson Commission observed that 'a problem of equity and fairness can scarcely arise as between political entities until such political entities have come into existence'. The Commission pointed out that during the period 1901–14, when the Protectorates of Northern and Southern Nigeria were administered separately, Northern Nigeria received financial contributions from Southern Nigeria in lieu of customs duties. The Commission found that 'the share of the total custom revenue which was generally at this time imputed to the North seems to have been round about 7 per cent.' Consequently, during the years 1908–13 the North received £70,000 each year out of a yearly average of £1,370,000 customs revenue collected at the ports of Southern Nigeria. The North clearly benefited from the development of the Southern ports although it did not contribute to the cost of developing these ports. Again, between 1914 and 1926, when there was partial amalgamation of North and South, the North – from the evidence of revenue allocation available to the Commission – was not unfairly treated; but thereafter, the North had been steadily under-equipped compared with the South, producing a serious deficiency in its educational facilities, and the Commission accordingly recommended a once-and-for-all capital grant to the North.

However, in spite of the Commission's finding that the North had less than its fair share of public funds and that the East had been treated more favourably than the North and the West, it rejected the demand for a full-scale application of the principle of derivation, on the ground that it was unsuitable for the kind of federal constitution envisaged by the General Conference. Instead, the Commission recommended a system of revenue allocation based on the combined principles of: (i) independent revenues, (ii) derivation, (iii) needs, and (iv) national interest.

Then, when the 1953 Constitutional Conference decided on a 'loose' federation, the issue of revenue allocation on the principle of derivation to the 'fullest degree' was reopened. The sole Fiscal Commissioner, Sir Louis Chick, observed in his report:

> Only the revenue collected by the Federal Government in excess of its own needs will be available for allocation according to the principle of derivation. It is necessary to mention this point because there appeared to be a tendency in one Region to regard the Federal Government as little more than the agent of the Regional Governments, and in another it was represented to me that the Federal Government should make a levy on the Regional Governments, within an agreed maximum, for the funds it needed to discharge its responsibilities. These views are inconsistent with that type of federal constitution proposed for Nigeria. The Federal Government is to be independent of the Regional Governments within its own sphere and coordinate with them. It will have its own definite responsibilities, and it must have its own revenues to discharge them. These commonly come from customs duties and income tax in other federations. When grants are made, it is the federal government that makes them to the regional governments and not the other way round. The further economic development of Nigeria will depend in large measure upon the financial resources of the Federal Government. If it is to have the necessary resources, its reasonable needs must be viewed generously and its

present reserves must not be distributed lavishly to the Regions. While it is true that the expensive social services are to be a Regional responsibility, it is also true that the main immediate need in the field of economic development is the improvement and extension of the country's road, railway, port and telecommunications facilities. These are to be Federal responsibilities and their improvement and extension will involve very heavy capital expenditure, part of which will have to be financed from loans. The financial strength of the Federal Government will be a weighty factor in determining the amounts and terms of loans, particularly when it becomes necessary to go outside Nigeria for them.

The Commissioner's discretion was, however, fettered by his terms of reference, and he was obliged to apply the principle of derivation to the fullest extent after allowing for the 'reasonable needs' of the Federal Government. The result of this allocation favoured the Western Region; but, as might be expected, this was a temporary advantage. Sir Louis Chick had warned in his report that the principle of derivation which he was obliged to apply to the fullest degree implied that the Regions were exchanging assured revenue for variable revenue. The Regional Governments would share in the improvement in Federal revenues resulting from development, but they would also share in the decline which would follow a fall in the value of Nigeria's foreign trade. Their finances would be less insulated than before from fluctuations in Nigeria's prosperity. This was a prophetic warning; for within four years of the Chick Report, the unsoundness of the principle of derivation was fully demonstrated.

The report of the 1958 Raisman Fiscal Commission castigated the principle of derivation in fairly strong terms, and urged that for the future the derivation formula should be abandoned because it entailed the distribution of large sums of money on the basis of 'calculations that can never be entirely accurate and which lend themselves to controversy'. Subsequent events proved the wisdom of not putting all the revenue eggs in the derivation basket. With the discovery of oil in commercial quantities in the East, that Region became much richer, contributing appreciably higher revenues to the national purse than it received.

By 1957, when the Raisman Fiscal Commission was set up, the Regions were aware of the disadvantages in a system of revenue allocation based wholly on the principle of derivation, and the

Commission's terms of reference were, therefore, more restrained in applying the principle. Indeed, the 1957 Conference stressed rather the principles of independent revenues and national needs, so that Sir Jeremy Raisman and his colleague, Mr R. C. Tress, were enabled to recommend a more rational system of allocation, which would ensure that all governments shared in each other's successes and setbacks. The Raisman formula became the basis of allocation for an independent Nigeria.

The main recommendation of the Raisman Commission was that

> the financial stability of the Federal Centre must be the main guarantee of the financial stability of Nigeria as a whole and that by its strength and solvency the credit-worthiness of the country will be apprais ed.

Therefore,

(i) the major sources of revenue – customs and excise duties and company income tax – must remain federal.

(ii) In order to accommodate the exercise of Regional jurisdiction in a field of jurisdiction which must of its nature be Federal, Regional Governments should have jurisdiction to impose sales taxes on produce, hides and skins, motor fuel, and diesel oil; and the Regions should exercise basic jurisdiction over personal income tax.

(iii) The Federal Government should exercise exclusive jurisdiction over mining and mineral taxation; but mining royalties and rents should be shared between the Region of their origin, the Federal Government, and all other Regions together, the last by way of a distributable pool.

(iv) 70 per cent of general import duty should be retained by the Federal Government, and 30 per cent should be paid into the distributable pool; the distributable pool, consisting of 30 per cent of the mining royalties and rents and 30 per cent of general import revenue, should be divided between the Regions in the following percentages: North, 40; West, 24; East, 31; Southern Cameroons, 5.

These recommendations were given statutory validity in the form of financial provisions in the Independence Constitution.

Sections 130 and 133 provided for the allocation of revenue derived from import duties, excise duties and export duties; Section 134 dealt with mining royalties and rents; and Section 135, with the allocation of funds in the distributable pool.

Section 164 of the Constitution provided for periodic reviews of the system of allocation, and the first of the Fiscal Reviews was undertaken in mid-1965 by Mr K. J. Binns, whose services were made available to Nigeria by the Australian Government. The Binns Commission was faced with the same arguments from the Regional Governments as had been urged before the Raisman Commission – that because Nigeria was a loose federation, greater financial autonomy should be given to the Regions. In rejecting this suggestion, the Commissioner quoted approvingly a statement by the renowned constitutional authority, Bryce: 'The problem which all federal nations have to solve is how to secure an efficient central government and preserve national unity.'

The difficulty of achieving the objective of a strong and efficient central government in the sphere of public finance was clearly one of the most serious problems of Nigerian federalism. All political parties in the country professed a common desire for a strong Federal Government; yet on every occasion that the exercise of revenue allocation was undertaken, the Federal Government lost vital revenue to the Regions. Of course, it was arguable that the Regional Governments bore a heavy burden for the provision of social services and therefore required far more money than their independent revenues could provide. But this argument ignored the crucial fact that in order to maintain full employment and promote the welfare and unity of Nigeria as a whole, the Federal Government had to be in a position to regulate overall economic and fiscal policy. Restriction of Federal discretion in this field could not but be detrimental to the economic progress of the Federation as a whole. Indeed, the late Federal Minister of Finance, in answer to criticisms of his financial and economic policies, pointed out that Nigeria's poor balance of payments position was in part due to the competitive industrialization programmes of the Regional Governments. Government spending, a high proportion of which was on social overheads, was increasing at the rate of almost ten per cent a year, or much faster than the overall growth rate of the economy as a whole.

But the Federal Government was under constant pressure to distribute its 'economic apples' more widely throughout the Federation without regard to economic sense or financial prudence. Because of Regional rivalries, the national project for the establishment of an iron and steel complex was to be distributed on a Regional basis against the best technical advice. As the late Federal Minister of Finance Chief Festus Okotie-Eboh put it: 'In a country of Nigeria's size, it is difficult to bring home to the ordinary citizen the extent of the industrial development taking place, unless it happens to be on his own doorstep. A man in Birnin Kebbi probably knows nothing of developments in, say, Calabar, and even if he did, he would be unimpressed because he can see no direct benefit to himself.' This attitude, unenlightened though it may be, is not without some justification. The man in Birnin Kebbi knows that the chance of his being offered employment in a cement factory at Calabar is remote, and so he expects his representative in parliament to secure a factory for Birnin Kebbi so as to ensure fair employment opportunities for the working population there.

In economic affairs, accordingly, the very wide constitutional powers of the Regions coupled with mounting inter-Regional rivalries and suspicions rendered national planning and direction ineffective. Manpower planning was severely limited by restrictive practices in the employment policies of the various governments, while education and social development suffered from the zeal with which each government guarded its constitutional rights. The result of all this was that there did not emerge identifiable national symbols able to attract the loyalty of the masses. But strong as were these centrifugal tendencies, the economic plight of the country itself promoted the growth of centripetal forces.

7. Social Implications of Public Policy

Educational

Unity in diversity is the most trenchant of the many clichés coined by the protagonists of a 'loose' federation for Nigeria, and in no sphere of governmental activity was the principle of diversity pursued to the same extent after federation as in education. Under the Federal Constitution education, at the primary and secondary level, was made a Regional responsibility, except that the Federal Government exercised Regional functions in the Federal Territory of Lagos, and might in addition make general education grants to Regional Governments. Higher education (including university, professional and technological education) was placed on the concurrent legislative list. Each of the governments maintained a number of teacher training institutions and technical colleges, and of the five existing universities, two were wholly financed by the Federal Government, and the other three jointly by the Federal Regional Governments. The Federal Government provided nearly 70 per cent of the financial requirements of higher education, but the Regional Governments bore a disproportionately heavier burden for primary and secondary education. The governments, no less than the people, attached such a high degree of importance to education that each Regional Government insisted on running an independent educational service complete with its own inspectorate. Machinery for joint consultation hardly existed.*

How effective this was will be considered below; but the fact that there were five distinct educational services in itself gave rise to considerable duplication of effort and much unnecessary expense. Indeed, a little over 20 per cent of the total annual budget of the country was devoted to education. No Regional Government spent less than 25 per cent of its budget on education,

* A Joint Consultative Committee on Education, comprising representatives of all five Ministries of Education, the Universities and the teaching profession, does exist; but its role in coordinating policy is negligible.

and the East and West, with universal primary education and one university institution in each, spent 45 per cent. The Northern Region embarked on a most ambitious programme for expanding secondary education and teacher training facilities in preparation for its programme of universal primary education, and the primary school population there nearly doubled within four years of independence, from 283,000 in 1960 to some 500,000 in 1964. Should universal primary education come into effect within the next four or five years in the North, primary school enrolments should rise rapidly there to the million mark and over. In the East, the annual rate of increase in primary school enrolments on the introduction of universal primary education was so steep that in 1961 the age of entry to primary school was raised from 5 to 6 years, and the length of the primary course shortened by one year; but even in spite of these measures, enrolments in the primary schools there remained fairly constant at about 1·3 million a year. The position in Western and Mid-Western Nigeria was similar, and the combined school enrolments in these two regions was running at 1·1 million. Altogether some 3 to 3·5 million children were enrolled in primary schools throughout Nigeria, and of these between 300,000 and 400,000 were leaving school each year, most of them unable to enter secondary or any other form of post-primary education.

There was, indeed, considerable expansion in the provision of facilities for secondary education throughout the Federation after independence. In 1960 there were 883 secondary grammar schools with a total enrolment of 135,434 pupils, and by 1963, the respective figures had become 1,245 and 211,879, with the rate of increase appearing likely to be sustained for a number of years. But compared with the rate of expansion in primary education, this was still relatively modest.[30] Consequently, every year a vast and growing number of primary school leavers entered the Nigerian labour market. Their seven or eight years in primary schooling having been devoted mainly to training in the three Rs, they had acquired no practical skills by the end of the course. They had neither the training nor the desire to take up agriculture or any skilled vocation, and sought paid employment in government and commercial establishments for which they were virtually disqualified by their level of education and in which opportunities were fast shrinking in relation to the number of qualified school leavers. Neither the primary school leavers themselves nor their peasant parents wanted a return to the traditional subsistence farming of the rural areas with all its drudgery and physical fatigue. Indeed, the long term economic policies of all the governments of the Federation were overtly directed towards a reduction in the very high proportion of the working population engaged in agriculture while at the same time raising the level of agricultural productivity. To this end all the Regional Governments, in addition to their efforts at industrialization, embarked on modest programmes of developing farm settlements, farm institutes and farmers' cooperatives. They stepped up their agricultural training programmes and extension services; but such was the nature and size of the problem that only a small proportion of primary school leavers could be absorbed into the existing programmes. The majority were drifting into the towns and fast becoming a solid unemployable community there, to provide the fodder for the political thuggery and lawlessness which appeared an increasingly commonplace feature of Nigerian political life. The dangers inherent in the growth of a large class of semi-literate, idle and dissatisfied young people cannot be exaggerated, and Nigerian politicians soon – if helplessly – began to recognize the threat which these young people presented to the stability of the country. All governments were anxious to solve the problem of mass unemployment among school leavers; but the steps they took could scarcely produce spectacular results.

Nigeria was, and is, faced with a serious dilemma. All enlightened Nigerians say they want the country to develop as a parliamentary democracy, and to achieve that goal there must be mass literacy in English (the lingua franca) in order to ensure the growth of public opinion, a prerequisite of parliamentary democracy. A very high proportion of public revenues (in addition to the very substantial private effort) is, therefore, regularly committed to education. This in turn reduces proportionately the percentage of public revenues that can be devoted to economic development. Educational expansion has outstripped the growth of the economy, with the inevitable result that the country cannot find remunerative employment for most of the products of universal primary education. To resolve this dilemma, Nigeria may have to take short-term measures which on the face of it appear to increase the very dangers against which she ought to guard. The masses of primary school leavers can and ought to be directed into activities which will increase the economic potential of the country. Their energies can be used in producing the infrastructure which economists agree has not yet built up anywhere near the level of self-sustaining growth. The country still needs many more and better roads than government is providing; there are vast land conservation and afforestation projects to tackle and other capital projects which require large sums of money but which can also be executed with a large labour force organized as a pioneer corps on a national scale. In some countries where this kind of experiment has been tried, it has taken on some of the features of a para-military organization, and to that extent it does present some danger to national security; but for the scheme to be effective, it has to be organized as a form of national service, through a disciplined force which should provide opportunities for remunerative work as well as training in vocational skills. To provide for this type of service, some funds will have to be diverted from existing industrial and educational projects. National service of this kind must provide trained manpower for the long-term programmes which are so necessary, so urgent.

If the problem of unemployment among primary school leavers is critical, it is not unique. Unemployment among the products of other levels of educational expansion also exists. Up to a few years ago, the overwhelming majority of secondary school leavers who did not go on to university secured paid employment within a few weeks of leaving school. But the situation has been completely altered by the rapid growth of the secondary school population since independence. Whereas the problem at the primary school level involves a complete lack of skills, the secondary school leaver's problem is a choice of vocation. He has the chance of further education in a post-school certificate technical institute or of paid employment as a white-collar worker in government, mercantile and industrial establishments. But this avenue of employment is, too, fast narrowing down, and the crush of white-collar job-seekers constantly grows.

On the other hand, no secondary school leaver with technical training has any difficulty in securing paid employment, because there is a critical shortage of technicians. Nigeria as a whole has lagged behind many other African countries in technical education. A commission appointed by the government of Eastern Nigeria in 1962 to review the educational policy of that Region, under the Chairmanship of Professor K. O. Dike, Vice-Chancellor of the University of Ibadan, noted that for every 100,000 of the population, there were at that time 621 taking technical education in Ghana, 245 in Sierra Leone, 217 in Gambia, and only 88 in Nigeria.[31] And these ratios have since changed to the disadvantage of Nigeria. This does not mean that in absolute terms Nigeria has fewer technicians than these countries, but the comparison underlines the size of the problem which Nigeria must face if it is successfully to industrialize its economy. In considering this problem, the Ashby Commission on post-secondary education, reporting in 1960, recommended that by 1970 Nigeria should be turning out 2,500 technicians a year in order to meet the national demand for this category of manpower. And the Federal Government itself declared that double this number will be required if the Nigerian economy is to achieve and maintain a four per cent growth rate. Yet the country is at present producing technicians at a rate well below the Ashby target, and there is every indication that it will fall far short of it even by 1970, let alone the Federal Government target of 5,000 a year.[32]

More recent manpower surveys conducted by the National Manpower Board of Nigeria indicate that the Ashby target has already been superseded by the actual demands in 1963, and that the probable demand in 1970 will be at least double that forecast in the Ashby Commission's report. Examination of the existing establishments reveals that at the intermediate foreman level there will be three vacancies for every qualified technician likely to be available by 1970. There already exists one Technical Institute in every one of the four Regions and a College of Technology in the Federal capital, but their combined enrolments in 1963–4 were 3,000, and their current total annual output of trained technicians is somewhere between 300 and 400, a figure well below the minimum requirement of the public sector alone. Many of the large commercial firms, public corporations and government technical establishments provide training courses for their employers as technicians and craftsmen, but although the facilities provided by these bodies are usually very good, enrolments are strictly related to the immediate vacancy position, and so maximum use is not made of the physical facilities available for training on a national scale.[33]

According to the manpower report cited:

> the number of persons sponsored for training under the various government scholarship and training programmes and by private employers, and who are likely to qualify for employment during the period 1963–8, totalled 15,472. The out-turn amounts to 15,146. The corresponding minimum additional needs for the period up to 1968 amount to 42,150, leaving a deficiency of 27,000. Thus out-turn from all sources is currently at a rate of about 3,000 per annum, as against an estimated average need of about 8,400 per annum.

The Manpower Board's 'intermediate' category is, of course, not limited to engineering technicians but includes all persons who are normally required to have had from at least one to two years specialized training after the G.C.E. (O level) or its equivalent – e.g. engineering assistants, laboratory technicians, agricultural superintendents and non-graduate teachers. It underlines the general shortages in this category of manpower.

In addition to the existing facilities for training technicians and craftsmen, there is provision in Nigeria's National Development Plan 1962–8 which, if fully implemented, should increase the annual output to about 1,000 technicians and 2,500 craftsmen by 1970. But this depends on a number of factors such as the availability of capital and qualified technical school teachers. Technical education is very expensive, both in terms of capital investment and qualified teachers, and Nigeria is short of such resources. The country's past uncoordinated efforts, with Federal and Regional Governments organizing their own educational services, have been wasteful in both capital resources and qualified teaching personnel. No technical institution at present makes maximum use of all its existing facilities because each (excepting the Federal institution) caters only for the youth of the Region which finances it, and each teaches almost the same courses as every other technical institute in the country. The cost in equipment and teaching staff of this multiplication is unnecessarily high and can be avoided if the Regions accept some specialization in the courses offered by the various Regional institutes on a reciprocal basis. Such an arrangement would maximize enrolments in each course and effect savings in money and qualified teachers. It would also ensure a national pattern for technical education. But after all this has been achieved, it will still be necessary to stimulate interest in technical training among the youth, particularly at the post-secondary school level. The traditional bias of secondary grammar school education towards entry into university has made the technical institute unattractive to students and their parents. The status symbol of a university degree is so much more alluring than that of a technician's diploma that grammar school boys will enter a technical institute only if it is impossible for them to get into a university, and even then most of them use their experience in the institute not as a preparation for intermediate level employment, but for entry to university. Why be a foreman of works if you can become an engineer ? In the past, the engineer attracted a disproportionately higher salary than the foreman. The gap between the two has narrowed considerably, but enrolments in technical institutes remain low.

This attitude to technical and vocational education is in part the legacy of our British connexions. Until very recently it was financially more rewarding to be a clerk than to be a plumber or a mechanic. The administrator is still more highly regarded than the agriculturist; and the debate is going on even now whether or not the university is a proper place to train the technicians needed by the country.

The same determination by the Regional Governments to exercise their constitutional right in education at the primary, secondary and technical levels was stretched to education at the university level. In October 1960 Nigeria possessed two university institutions (one of them only a few weeks old) with a total enrolment of 1,400 students. Today it possesses five universities, with an enrolment of 7,500. In June 1960, only 184 students obtained first degrees from Nigerian institutions of higher education. In June 1965 the number of first degrees awarded by Nigerian universities rose to 1,200. Three of the five universities were sponsored by Regional Governments, and were then jointly financed by the Federal and Regional Governments, while the other two were wholly financed by the Federal Government, with a total annual subvention of £6·5 million. The universities were, thus, receiving nearly 27 per cent of the national education budget.

This impressive rate of expansion in higher education naturally began to cause some anxiety, and at the end of the 1964–5 academic year a number of Nigerian newspapers gave wide publicity to the dangers in over-production of graduates and the possibility of graduate unemployment, with all the social problems which might arise from such a situation. But the present rate of graduate output is still below the Ashby Commission's projections of 2,000 graduates a year by 1970 to meet the high-level manpower needs of the country during the '70s. The Ashby Commission considered the output of 2,000 graduates a year to be a first and modest objective, for the Commission itself felt that even after graduates had been produced at that rate for ten years, Nigeria would still have fewer graduates per thousand of the population then either Egypt or Ghana. And this projection was made on the basis of a population estimate of 44 million. For a population of 55·6 million, the disparity is even greater. But, of course, the Ashby Commission carefully considered the proportions of the different categories of graduates that ought to be produced – teachers, engineers, doctors, agriculturists, veterinarians, economists, accountants, and so forth. The distribution of graduates over fields of study or professions in any one year ought to be of far more concern than the total number of graduates, not only to government but to the public in general. In 1964, of 708 students who graduated from Nigerian universities, only 28 obtained degrees in Agriculture, 34 in Medicine, 54 in Engineering and Architecture, 129 in pure Science. The remaining 453 obtained degrees in Arts and the Social Sciences. This means that some 65 per cent of students graduating in 1964 obtained degrees in the Humanities, compared with 35 per cent in Physical Sciences.[34] And this pattern of distribution is the complete reverse of that recommended by the Ashby Commission.

The National Universities Commission, the body charged with responsibility for the coordination of university development, has been exhorting the universities to increase their enrolments in the Science departments and stop any further expansion in the Humanities. The 1965 output of graduates has shown some slight change in favour of the Sciences, but the universities by themselves cannot achieve the desired results. The root of the problem lies in the serious weakness of secondary school Science, which only the concerned effort of government can cure. Most secondary grammar schools do not have enough money to equip good science laboratories and employ qualified science teachers; so, while the number of sixth form students is increasing yearly by leaps and bounds, only a tiny proportion of the product has sufficient training in Science. Each year thousands of secondary school leavers apply to enter the universities, but only a few of them have the basic qualification for enrolment in the Science and Technology departments of universities. The universities are doing their best to provide remedial courses, but the size of the problem calls for a 'crash' programme on a national basis. In place of the widely dispersed individual efforts of the Regional authorities, the country requires a concentration of a few – say, one in each Region – very large Sixth Form Science Schools on the same lines as the Federal School of Science in Lagos, with enrolments of at least 1,000 in each school to meet the needs of the universities and technical colleges. A programme of this nature can best be promoted by the Federal Ministry of Education working in cooperation with the Regional Ministries. Indeed, in the entire field of education only cooperative federalism can ensure that the people of Nigeria will derive the maximum benefit from the high financial sacrifice which is being made on their behalf. No Regional government in present circumstances can by itself give the people within its jurisdiction adequate facilities for education at all levels, nor can the country afford the expensive multiplication of facilities characteristic of a 'loose' federation. At the time of federation and the inauguration of Regional self-government, the Regional Governments had at their disposal large financial resources from the accumulated reserves of the Marketing Boards. These reserves have since been seriously run down, and no Regional Government is any longer financially able to develop and maintain a completely separate educational system of its own without detracting from the standard and quality of its own public services.

The Moral Problem

Everybody expects the government to provide modern social

amenities – good roads, pipe-borne water, hospitals, schools, electricity, and police services. Few expect the government to provide sound moral leadership. When roads and bridges are washed away by the rains, the public exhort the government to replace them. If there are persistent power failures or overcrowding in schools and hospitals or an outbreak of thuggery, the government and their agencies are urged to act promptly to remedy the situation. But when the general standard of public morality falls visibly, the Church, the schools and the parents, not the government, are blamed for losing their authority over the new generation. No one calls upon the government to do anything about it, even though current public attitudes are to a very great extent conditioned by the public policies of the government.

In Nigeria not only have public attitudes to such issues as tribalism, nepotism, bribery and corruption been conditioned by the actual practices of governments (as distinct from their declared policies), but attitudes to public property, to public service and to national unity have been profoundly affected by the public policies pursued by the various governments of the Federation. A political party which comes to office by appealing to the tribal loyalty of the majority of voters in the numerically dominant group is obliged to put the material interests of that dominant group before those of any other citizens. As a government, it cannot but allow its policies to be coloured by tribalism and nepotism. If the leaders of the governing party in a Region can threaten with impunity to deny social amenities to any constituency which fails to return the government party's candidate at an election, then a fair and free election is impossible. Yet these were commonplace practices of the governing parties in post-independence Nigeria, despite their declared policies of opposition to tribalism, nepotism and corruption. Occasionally a newspaper headline cried out against 'these undemocratic practices', but the protest came from an opposition organ, and so that was the end of the matter. Most Nigerians who read these protests shook their heads disapprovingly, but shrugged the matter from their minds. 'It is politics,' they said, and in politics 'the end justifies the means.'

Prior to the Second World War, participation in Nigerian

public affairs at the national level was a privilege and duty exercised almost exclusively by the tiny professional elite of lawyers, doctors and 'merchant-princes' in Lagos, Calabar and Abeokuta. Local affairs were largely in the hands of illiterate traditional leaders who accepted without demur the guiding hand of the paternalistic District Officer. The British-educated elite, Victorian to the core, accepted without any reservation the norms of British public life and the power-structure of a British dependency. Then came the postwar nationalist mass movement, which wrenched political leadership from the professional elite. The new political leaders had a more varied educational background. Some of them had studied in North America, others in Britain, but most of them were educated locally and were either veterans of the Second World War or leaders of the developing trade union movement. These new leaders, closely linked with the politically conscious urban masses, did not feel bound by the same restraints as their Victorian predecessors, and as their political influence increased, their dependence on intellectual or ideological arguments in support of self-government diminished. The old elite were denounced as 'Uncle Toms' and accused of feathering their own nests at the expense of the toiling masses. If any son or daughter of a member of the old elite won a government scholarship, it was not earned on merit, but on privilege. It was all part of the 'fruits of office', which would descend to the nationalists once the goal of self-government was attained. The masses were led to expect that self-government would bring freedom from restraint to a degree which would in fact have been quite inconsistent with the achievement of true nationhood. These expectations proved to be unrealizable, but the mental attitudes engendered by them linger on. During the hey-day of the struggle against colonial rule, it was fashionable to show little respect for constituted authority. It was a singular act of patriotism for a young clerk to refuse to do a 'day's job for his keep', because conscientious service to the colonial masters would perpetuate the system. Unfortunately for the country, at independence the Nigerian heirs of imperial mastery took over the system intact. Soon after the honeymoon of the independence celebrations, the masses came to learn that the promise was very different from the fulfilment.

The new rulers, their kith and kin, proved even more fallible that their foreign predecessors, being, like the masses who voted them into power, the products of a traditional social system which is difficult to fit into an individualistic European political and economic system. In the traditional small-scale closed African society, every man is his brother's keeper. He has a duty to succour his relatives; and in the more complex stratified society of the Moslem areas in the North, this duty extends beyond the kin-group. There a man has a duty not only to his relatives and dependants but to his followers and all those who place themselves under his protection. A person of wealth and high status (and both almost always go together in Nigerian traditional society) is expected to dispense largesse to his relatives, friends and followers. And the conspicuous consumption of goods is a recognized traditional means of expressing status and wealth. In the absence of a money economy and banks, how else does a man spend the surplus of yams he has harvested than to 'cook food' for his townspeople? Nigerian Ministers succeeded to the legacy of power, status and wealth left by the British. They were, therefore, expected by many of their compatriots to behave as men of wealth, power and status in the traditional sense: to provide for their relatives and dispense largesse to their political supporters. No one seemed concerned about the source of wealth for fulfilling these obligations. Most of the first set of Ministers under the Macpherson Constitution fell an easy prey to their political opponents and detractors in 1953, because they were too steeped in textbook idealism to appreciate this simple fact. It then required very little effort to discredit a Minister amongst his constituents and political supporters by telling them that he was appointed to office so that he might build them a hospital, secure appointments for them on the boards of government-sponsored corporations, and have their business interests promoted regardless of personal merit. He had not done any of these things and must be removed from office. And, of course, it was easy to quote numerous precedents from other countries to support this 'spoils system' of government as the justified enjoyment of office. Whether the generality of Nigerians approved the 'spoils system' or not, they condoned it at the most critical period in the development of parliamentary democracy in Nigeria. In 1957 the electorate in one of the Regions overwhelmingly defeated an attempt by the opposition parties to prevent the public funds of the Region from being invested in the private, unlicensed bank of a leading politician. Since that event the fight against the 'spoils system' increasingly appeared a lost cause, only kept alive on the pages of the newspapers.

Tribalism, nepotism, bribery and corruption threatened increasingly to defeat all endeavours to establish a just and efficient administration. Every Nigerian admitted with anger, shame or embarrassment that these evils existed. Hardly a day passed without some politician, great or small, being reported in the Nigerian press as having appealed to some local council members, secondary school pupils or debating society to eschew these evils. And hardly a day passed but some Regional leader appealed for 'unity and solidarity' among the members of his tribal group. 'Anti-Bribery Societies' sprang up here and there in the country. The police formed X-Squads to fight bribery and corruption in the force. Yet in spite of all these public efforts, the evils continued to thrive. One reason is that we condemn these abuses when they are perpetrated by individuals but connive at them when perpetrated by a group of people in authority. In their classic study of *Corruption in Developing Countries*,[35] Wraith and Simpkins noted the difficulty of trying to write about corruption in high places – at the Federal and Regional Government level – even though everybody knew or believed that corruption was rampant there. The two authors, therefore, turned the searchlight of their inquiry on corruption at a lower level, and concluded that 'local government in the Southern Regions of Nigeria has reached the point of being a conspiracy against the public, so riddled is it with bribery, nepotism, politics and corruption'.

Corruption at this level, indeed, was fully documented by successive commissions of inquiry appointed by the Regional Governments. But then it was easy in Nigeria to express righteous indignation against those in a subordinate position. It was not so easy to be indignant with colleagues, and not easy at all to protest at the conduct of superiors. The honest local councillor only whispered about the dishonesty of his colleagues until the Regional Government was persuaded by press publicity to appoint a commission of inquiry into allegations of corruption against the council. The Minister who was a man of integrity (and there were many) suffered in silence the predatory abuse of office by his irresponsible colleagues, in the name of Cabinet solidarity. The newspaper editor who roundly condemned corruption in high places kept mute when his political patron was associated with an outrageous act of swindling the public.

In a postscript to their 'glimpses of corruption', Wraith and Simpkins referred to the Report of a Commission of Inquiry into the Statutory Corporations of the Western Region of Nigeria. The Report alleged that:

> a political party systematically transferred large sums of public money to its own use through the device of a so-called Investment and Properties Corporation, a large part of which was spent on electioneering; and that considerable personal benefits were obtained by highly placed individuals, who were able to obtain the money with little or no regard for the normal controls over public expenditure.

It was not difficult for the political party to challenge the report as being biased, because it was a matter of common knowledge that the governing parties in all the Regions were guilty of similar, if not identical, practices, and because at the time of the Inquiry the particular political party so criticized had excited the hot hostility of the then Federal Government. As long as a party, government, council or other group of individuals was in tune with its superior authority, its acts, even if blatantly exceptionable, were not publicly condemned. Opportunity was, therefore, provided for fantastic gossip, for exaggeration and distortion. Corruption fed on itself. The lurid stories about the dishonestly acquired wealth of many Nigerian public men had their origin in this attitude of 'turning a blind eye' to the misdeeds of friends and compatriots in the hope of avoiding public embarrassment.

It is traditional in all Nigerian cultural groups to support, fight for and protect a member of one's in-group against attacks by outsiders; but it is also a common cultural trait in Nigerian tribal life that cheating and all forms of dishonest acts directed against members of one's group are condemned and subjected to the most severe group sanctions. Nigerians of today have to learn to accept for all purposes that the entity called Nigeria must replace the traditional tribal or cultural group. Acts of dishonesty by public men must therefore be seen as directed against the in-group of which they are members, and as deserving, therefore, of the severest public sanctions. Until the average member of present-day Nigerian society is willing to employ some immediate sanction against the person who deviates from the universally accepted standard of integrity, it will be impossible to contain, let alone eliminate, corruption and nepotism in our public life. National integration or unity will only be achieved by the acceptance of the nation-state as the depository of all political power. And acceptance of this concept depends in turn on the determination of those in authority to give moral leadership to the public. The notion of political office as a means of acquiring wealth or personal power is incompatible with parliamentary democracy.

Unhappily, many otherwise perfectly honest Nigerians tend to accept or condone the quite untraditional concept of entering public service with the sole aim of personal enrichment, claiming it as the 'African way of life'. But while this statement is generally valid in the political sphere of our public life, the same cannot, happily, be said of the higher civil service. There is no doubt that a few highly placed civil servants have taken advantage of their position of influence to benefit themselves materially; but by and large, the top cadre of Nigerian civil servants has fought hard to maintain the standard of integrity bequeathed by the British colonial administrators. The sweeping allegation of corruption in high places so often made against them was unjust to a group of young men who discharged responsibilities – in general, most creditably – for which they had the barest minimum of practical training before independence. The danger for the country is that overworked, as most of them are, and unsupported by adequate technical advice from below, they could succumb to political pressures from above. One protection against this danger is for them to maintain a high degree of functional interdependence with one another, however many distinct governments they might be required to serve. For them Nigeria, not the particular Region in which they are serving, ought to be the unit of administration or the economic compass. Their concentration on one section of that unit ought to be accepted as a mere division of labour, directed towards rapid economic development and the achievement of a fully integrated nation. Amidst the dust and thunder of political strife, only the civil service can ensure the achievement of functional unity.

The Problem of Social Inequality

Some of the public policies pursued by the various governments of the Federation produced, however undesignedly, social inequalities. It was the declared policy of all governments to raise the living standards of the people as a whole; to foster economic growth not only by direct participation in industrial development but by encouraging Nigerian enterprise. Because there was very little indigenous private capital, the governments sponsored institutions out of public funds for the purpose of financing indigenous private business; because expatriate banks would not take the risk of extending credit facilities to Nigerian entrepreneurs, government-sponsored banks were established to 'liberalize credit facilities' for Nigerian businessmen. The Regional Development Corporations, Finance Corporations, Agricultural Credit Banks and, more recently, the Nigerian Industrial Development Bank (jointly sponsored by the Central Bank of Nigeria and the International Finance Corporation) were all financial institutions established out of public funds to provide long- and medium-term finance for the private sector of the economy. Some of them successfully executed a number of viable agricultural and medium-scale industrial projects. All of them suffered in their loan policies from too much political control. They were often obliged to make loans to individuals on grounds other than simple economic criteria and with very little assurance or prospect that the loans would be recovered. Many borrowers applied loan monies to purposes other than those for which the loans were made.

The most common form of investment was into residential housing, for urban housing, amongst all investments, yielded the highest dividends in the shortest possible time. Investment in housing was therefore widely preferred to that in productive enterprises. And as if the abnormally high rents derivable were not sufficient compensation, all governments shied away from introducing a property tax on residential houses, despite the high cost of developing urban land for residential purposes. There thus rapidly grew up a new class of wealthy absentee landlords, who owed their position to their political affiliations and the public purse. It was mainly to this class that Nigeria owed her reputation among overseas visitors for good-humoured leisureliness, prestigious American cars, and lavish entertainment in the midst of poverty and unemployment.

On the other hand, the salary- and wage-earners, whose standard of living fell by comparison with that of the *nouveaux riches*, continually agitated for the introduction of rent-control by the governments. The issue of rent-control became so vital to the wider problem of living standards, indeed, that since 1947 no government Commission of Inquiry into salary and service conditions failed to comment on it and to urge the building of more and more low-cost houses by the governments and their agencies. The governments accepted such proposals and provided some housing; but because of its many commitments, no government found enough money to provide an adequate number of workers with residential estates, a situation which made it all the more deplorable that speculative building was not taxed as a source of supplementary revenue for low-cost housing estates. Certainly, to the extent that a tiny minority were enabled to acquire wealth out of public funds, there was a provocative widening of the gap between the rich and the poor. A policy whose avowed object was the very laudable one of increasing private Nigerian participation in national economic growth excited, through unhealthy social forces, an unexpected new tension, which undermined productive relations between employers and employees, and between governments and trade unions. Every Salary Review Commission since 1941 (and there were seven between 1941 and 1964) resulted in an upward rise in salaries and wages; yet the relative gap between the rich (including politicians, administrators, top managers of business) and the ruled (the huge peasant population, the junior workers and wage-earners) seemed hardly to be affected by this progressive improvement in the wage system of the country.

That the governments were alive to this persisting problem is shown by the terms of reference for the latest of the Salary

Review Commissions, the Morgan Commission, appointed in 1963:

(i) To investigate the existing wage structure, remuneration and conditions of service in wage-earning employments in the country and to make recommendations concerning a suitable new structure, as well as adequate machinery for a wages review on a continuing basis; (ii) To examine the need for (*a*) general upward revision of salaries and wages of junior employees in both government and private establishments, (*b*) the abolition of a daily-wage system, and (*c*) the introduction of a national minimum wage, and to make recommendations.

In its report the Commission recommended a 'national minimum wage' based upon the principle of a 'living wage', fixing of which, the Commission claimed, should take into account not only estimates of the income required by the individual to live at a minimum standard of health and decency, but also the individual's other needs, including family responsibilities, amusement and leisure. In rejecting this particular recommendation the Federal Government pointed out, with considerable justification, that the 'living wage' had to be related to 'the ability of employers to pay; the possibility of further price increases; and the effect on farmers and the peasants generally, who constitute about eighty per cent of the country's population'.

The last ground of objection – the effect on the peasant population – was the most valid of all the objections, for the gap between the wage-earning population and the peasantry was – and is – if anything wider than that between the top managers and administrators and the wage-earners, and to that extent all salaried persons and wage-earners belong to the privileged minority of the population. All development planning has favoured the salaried and wage-earning populations who reside in the cities and towns. The modern social services, the industrial projects and all those government policies which enable Nigerians to increase their earning capacity have so far been concentrated in the towns. The problem of rural development has been a hardy annual in the debating chambers of all Nigerian legislatures; but in spite of the generally recognized need to improve and expand agricultural production, the practical outcome of public policy has been a relative lowering of peasant living standards compared with those of the wage-earners. Inevitably every wage-increase has been accompanied by a corresponding rise in the price of local food-stuffs. It will be comparatively easy further to narrow the gap in the level of income between the top administrators and the lower-income wage-earners by abolishing the fringe benefits which the former enjoy by virtue of office; but a permanent increase in the latters' real earnings will only begin to develop when conditions in the rural areas improve sufficiently to facilitate expansion of primary production and the development of an urban-industrial exchange in primary products.

8. The Crisis of Unity

Concerning the exercise of their executive authority by the various units of the Federation, the constitution made formal provision to ensure the continuance of the Federation; thus Section 80 of the Constitutional Order-in-Council, 1960, provided that the executive authority of a Region 'shall be so exercised as not to impede or prejudice the exercise of the executive authority of the Federation or to endanger the continuance of federal government in Nigeria'. If any Region exercised its executive authority in a manner which contravened the provisions of Section 80, Parliament had power to act under Section 66(1) of the Constitution, which provided that:

> During any period in which there is in force a resolution of each House of Parliament supported by the votes of not less than two-thirds of all the members of that House declaring that the executive authority of a Region is being exercised in contravention of Section 80 of this Constitution, Parliament may make laws for that Region with respect to matters not included in the Legislative Lists to such an extent as may appear to Parliament to be necessary for securing complaisance with the provisions of that section.

Such constitutional provisions not only ensured that no Region of the Federation might secede, but that no Regional Government could pursue policies patently inimical to the interests of the Federation as a whole, except with the acquiescence of the Federal Government, or of the overwhelming majority of the members of both Houses of Parliament. A Regional Government which openly pursued policies out of step with the overall interests of the Federation or which attempted to secede from the Federation rendered itself liable to dismissal by Parliament at the request of the Federal Government. Far more seriously, by securing an affirmative vote in both Houses of Parliament for declaring a

State of Emergency, the Federal Government could not only dismiss a recalcitrant Regional Government, but in exercise of its emergency powers suspend the provisions of the constitution relating to fundamental human rights during the period of the emergency. Section 65(1) of the Constitution provided that:

> Parliament may at any time make such laws for Nigeria or any part thereof with respect to matters not included in the Legislative Lists as may appear to Parliament to be necessary or expedient for the purposes of maintaining or securing peace, order and good government during any period of emergency;

and Section 65(3) defined 'period of emergency' as any period during which

> (*a*) the Federation is at war; (*b*) there is in force a resolution passed by each House of Parliament declaring that a state of public emergency exists; or (*c*) there is in force a resolution passed by each House of Parliament supported by the votes of not less than two-thirds of all the members of the House declaring that democratic institutions in Nigeria are threatened by subversion.

The provisions embodied in both Sections 65 and 66 of the Constitution were of the most profound significance not only for the continuation of federal government, but for establishing the constitutional supremacy of the Federal Government. In the last resort the will of the Federal authority – executive and legislative – must override that of the component units if federation was to endure; but this imposed an onerous responsibility on the Federal authority to exercise its will with care and responsibility.

In May 1962, the provisions of Section 65 were invoked against the Action Group Government in Western Nigeria. The proximate cause of the action by the Federal Government was a feud within the Action Group, the governing party in the Region, as a result of which Chief S. L. Akintola, the Deputy Leader of the Party and Premier of Western Nigeria, was deposed from his party office and asked to resign his appointment as Premier of the Region. He refused, whereupon a majority of members of the Western House of Assembly (who were all members of the Action Group) signed a petition to the Governor of the Region withdrawing their support from Chief Akintola as Premier and praying the Governor to exercise his powers under Section 33(10)(a) of the Constitution of Western Nigeria to remove Chief Akintola from the office of Premier. That section of the Constitution provides that 'the Governor shall not remove the Premier from office unless it appears to him that the Premier no longer commands the support of a majority of the members of the House of Assembly.' On the receipt of the petition signed by a majority of the members of the House of Assembly, the Governor revoked Chief Akintola's appointment as Premier and proceeded to appoint Chief D. S. Adegbenro as Premier in his stead. Chief Akintola challenged the legality of the Governor's action in the High Court of Western Nigeria, but the Court transferred the issue to the Supreme Court. Meanwhile, Chief Akintola advised the Governor to dissolve the Legislative Houses of the Region. The Governor refused; and when a meeting of the House of Assembly was summoned by the Governor, violence and disorder broke out, ending only when the Police dispersed the members with tear gas and locked up the Chamber of the House.

A few days after these events, and before the Courts determined the legality of the Governor's action, the Federal Government intervened, and Parliament passed a resolution, by the provisions of Section 65 (3) (b), declaring that a State of Public Emergency existed in Nigeria. The debate on the motion asking the House to adopt the resolution turned on the interpretation given to the phrase 'State of Emergency' by the Federal Government. The Prime Minister, who moved the motion, urged that it was impossible to carry on the public affairs of Western Nigeria 'in an atmosphere of warring factions of the party in power so sadly rent asunder'. He considered that, in these circumstances, there was no validly constituted Government in Western Nigeria, and 'no responsible Government of the Federation could allow an explosive situation such as that which now exists in Western Nigeria to continue without taking adequate measures to ensure that there is an early return to the Region of peace, order and good government.'

The Leader of the Opposition, Chief Obafemi Awolowo, however, thought that 'a State of Public Emergency arises only when there is widespread violence in any part of the Federation or in the whole of the Federation.' He said there was no violence outside the Chamber of the legislature, and that the rest of the

Region was peaceful. He warned that it would be an act of bad faith if Parliament suspended the constitution of a Region merely because a minority of the members of that Region's legislature decided to impose their will on the legislature or impede its proceedings.

In the event, however, two-thirds of the members of Parliament accepted the view that the existence of 'an explosive situation' following a split within the party in power was sufficient evidence of a 'State of Public Emergency', and so allowed the Federal Government to exercise its powers under the Emergency Powers Act, 1961. Some of the emergency measures which were taken under this Act were challenged in Court; but the Courts made clear that they regarded the issue as one necessarily based on political judgement and, therefore, one within the competence of Parliament. For instance, in its ruling on a motion by Chief Adegbenro, seeking a court order that his detention by the Administrator for Western Nigeria appointed under the Emergency Regulations was unlawful, the Federal Supreme Court remarked:

> ... We, however, feel that, on the question of whether or not there were sufficient grounds for Parliament to declare a state of emergency, it is unnecessary for us to rule on the submission that if Parliament acted *mala fide* in making a declaration of a state of public emergency, the Court could hold it invalid, since it is impossible to say in the present case that there was no ground to justify a declaration; it is not for the Court to go outside the provisions of Section 65(3) of the Constitution of the Federation defining emergency.[36]

Without going into the merits of the Federal Government's arguments in this particular case, it is sufficient to stress that the Federal authority had constitutional powers to intervene in the affairs of any Region of the Federation, not only to maintain peace, order and good government (if, in the judgement of the Federal authority, peace, order and good government had broken down), but also to coerce a recalcitrant Regional authority to exercise its powers in a manner which would ensure the continuance of federal government in Nigeria.

All the formal provisions outlined above were effective in promoting centripetal tendencies only to the extent that the different units of the Federation whole-heartedly cooperated to make the arrangements work, and to the extent that the Federal authority exercised the powers conferred upon it by the Constitution with a clear concern for the effect on national unity. In a Federal Cabinet which was a coalition of Regional interests, enforcement of constitutional powers and duties could be an extremely difficult exercise in political judgement, depending upon which particular combination of Regional interests controlled the Federal Cabinet. In 1962, the parties in coalition in the Federal Cabinet were the N.P.C. (representing Northern Regional interests) and the N.C.N.C. (predominantly Eastern). The Action Group which was in control of the Government of the West constituted the Federal Parliamentary Opposition. It was, therefore, relatively easy for the Federal authority to discharge its constitutional duties in connexion with the 'explosive situation' in that Region. It was also not without its dangers.

Fortunately for Nigerian unity, there are a number of informal centripetal factors which transcend Regional boundaries. Foremost amongst them is the trade union movement. Unlike their counterparts in many other parts of the world, Nigerian wage-earners did not have to fight hard for the right to form genuinely free trade unions. Indeed, they were encouraged by the Colonial Government to organize themselves into unions, according to their choice. The consequences of this policy have not been altogether happy. The practice of trade unionism in Nigeria has often fallen far short of its principles. There have been serious structural and organizational problems, defective leadership, and lack of discipline in the rank and file of the membership, all of which have weakened the collective bargaining power of the unions. But union membership *has* cut across tribal and political divisions, establishing an allegiance more nationally directed than is the case with any other organized group. In spite of the incessant personal and bitter struggle for leadership among the top union members, the unions themselves have constituted the only organized group in which tribal affiliation has never been made the basis for leadership and status. Indeed, the trade unions demonstrated their potential as a national force when they successfully organized a nation-wide strike in July 1964, paralysing within a few days the entire life of the Federation. After a week, all the five Governments were obliged to call a truce and negotiate a settlement. The lesson of their strength in united action could not have been lost on the trade unions, and if this strength is channelled along constructive lines it could prove a tremendous force for the unity of the country.

English, the lingua franca of the literate community, continues to be a powerful factor in producing national consciousness. At present it is the principal medium through which the various facets of Nigerian culture, both past and present, and of Nigerian opinion are disseminated. Nigerian legal and parliamentary institutions, which reflect the British heritage, have been a strong centralizing influence and, as will be shown below, every thoughtless departure from the framework of these institutions has shaken the fonndations of Nigerian unity.

When Lagos became a British colony, English Common Law was introduced, and on the establishment of the Protectorates of Northern and Southern Nigeria, the Law was extended to the two Protectorates under the provision that 'the rules of the English Common Law, the principles of equity and the statutes of general application in England, as at 1 January 1960, shall henceforth apply', except that the indigenous laws and customs of the country were given statutory recognition, provided that they were not repugnant to the principles of natural justice, equity and good conscience and were not inconsistent with any valid local enactment. In consequence of this provision, there have developed over the years some general principles of Nigerian civil and criminal law to which all Nigerian citizens are subject. Commercial and industrial transactions, in particular, have been the main fields where English law has almost completely superseded the indigenous systems and unified the government of economic relations between persons of different tribes and differing religions. English legal traditions have engendered among the younger Nigerians a belief in the rule of law, equality before the law, and respect for the dignity of the individual. These ideas were given statutory sanction in the constitutional provisions dealing with fundamental rights, the independence of the judiciary and of the Director of Public Prosecutions. But constitutional amendments were subsequently introduced abolishing the Judicial Service Commission, the body which nominated judges for appointment, and making the Director of Public Prosecutions answerable to a politically appointed Attorney-

General. These changes caused serious misgivings amongst many Nigerians. Whatever arguments were advanced in support of such departures convinced few that their freedom and equality under the law were not being eroded.

The last, and perhaps the most important, of the centripetal forces was the parliamentary system itself, which had been unanimously adopted by all Nigeria's political leaders. Representative government is the basis of social control everywhere in indigenous Nigerian societies. From the most segmentary political system found in an Eastern Ibo or Tiv village to the oligarchy of a Yoruba kingdom or the centralized feudal emirate, the underlying principle of political organization is representation of vested interests. The interest-groups may be based on kinship, on ritual functions, or on occupational categories; but all types of indigenous political systems have promoted government by discussion and decision by majority. What has been alien to Nigerians is large-scale organization. Advocates of a single-party system for the newly independent African countries have often argued that the two-party or multi-party system is an alien political concept. This view is quite contrary to the facts of indigenous African political organization. Anyone who watches a traditional village meeting cannot but notice that decisions are reached only after exhaustive argument in which oratory often wins the day. Nigerian folklore, indeed, abounds with tales of factional intrigues in the Chief's court and the control of the Chief's conscience by the wily courtier who gathers round himself the more powerful faction of the village community. These traditional social situations transplanted to modern soil produce political sections or parties. The present generation of Nigerians enjoys argument and opposition to the established order as much as did its forebears.

Parliamentary government offered a very satisfying substitute for village oratory, opposition to constituted authority, and some opportunity for organized intrigue against those in office. Above all else, it was through Parliament that the corporate will of Nigeria as a nation was expressed. Many Nigerians, to be sure, would have liked to see Parliament sit more often, discuss international affairs more seriously, and scrutinize the policies and actions of government departments more closely. When Parliament met, crowds gathered in the immediate area, not so much to follow the proceedings as to feel the attachment to Parliament as the embodiment of the nation's will.

Yet in spite of these elaborate arrangements and formal institutions for promoting national unity, it must be admitted that the trends of the last fifteen years nourished separation rather than unity. Each Regional Government was more concerned with standing on its constitutional rights and promoting its particular interests than with promoting the overall interests of the nation. And the country developed no national symbols strong enough to supersede existing Regional loyalties. Regional leaders did not accept whole-heartedly the idea of the nation-state as the legitimate depository of political power. Parliamentary democracy on the Western model was weak and ineffectual. The legislatures possessed all the outward trappings of a British-type parliamentary institution – Speaker, Mace, Government and Opposition Benches, Whips; even the oratory and the cut and thrust of parliamentary debates abundantly existed, but the spirit of political tolerance which springs from the mutual desire of government and opposition for security against arbitrary political power was noticeably absent in the proceedings of every legislature in the land. Instead, the legislature tended more and more to become the rubber stamp of the executive and the party. Federal members of parliament seemed content to sit as the Regional delegates of the party on whose tickets they had been returned, and in the Regional legislatures themselves organized opposition had all but disappeared.

These trends raised doubts in many minds over the prospects or relevance of parliamentary democracy in Nigeria and even of the continuance of federal government at all. Some people thought that democracy is a luxury which only advanced nations can afford. They maintained that a country like Nigeria lacks the degree of ethnic and linguistic unity, and the standard of literacy and technical development which are the prerequisites of a modern parliamentary democracy. But though cultural homogeneity and technological advance certainly facilitate the practice of modern parliamentary democracy where they exist in combination with other predisposing factors, such as the tradition of government by discussion and compromise, they will not in themselves ensure the survival of a democratic system. Some of the technologically most advanced countries in Europe have failed to sustain genuine parliamentary democracy. On the other hand, many former British colonies and dependencies operated a limited parliamentary system (internal self-government) for some years before the 'steel frame' of the British Colonial Office was withdrawn. Nigeria, indeed, operated such a parliamentary system for nearly ten years before independence, during which period Nigerian Ministers and politicians were subjected to the same discipline and code of public conduct as are British Ministers of State.

The relaxation following independence of the rules for the conduct of public affairs was a major contributing factor to the weakness of the parliamentary system in Nigeria, as was the unregulated desirc for power. It is true that those Nigerian political leaders who sponsored the movement for a 'loose' federation were genuinely concerned for the special interests of their ethnic group or Regional political unit; but they were equally concerned for the possession of personal political power. And political control of the Federal authority was, in the circumstances of the time, extremely difficult. If, therefore, they could not control the Centre, they demanded that as much power and as much revenue as possible should be taken away from it so as to neutralize without actually destroying it. The result of this policy was the increasing determination of the parties dominating the various Regions to entrench themselves at home so firmly that they were assured of controlling the Regional Government indefinitely. And the control of a Regional Government not only ensured power within the Region itself, but also determined the distribution of seats in the Federal Parliament. In a Region where the government and party were synonymous, the result of an election, whether Regional or Federal, was usually a foregone conclusion. The Government was always able to manipulate the electoral machinery to its advantage; but as no Regional Government was able to command majority support in every one of the constituencies within its area of jurisdiction, it exercised its power in such a way as to perpetuate itself in office indefinitely. Constituencies that persisted in returning opposition candidates were denied social services; their traditional leaders were humiliated, and opposition party activists were mulcted by punitive taxes; marginal constituencies were won over by favourable treatment in the provision of social services – pipe-borne water, electric lights, tarred roads, hospitals – which ought to have been every tax-paying community's right, whether it voted for the government party candidate or not. Under the Nigerian electoral regulations, it was no offence for a spokesman of the government party to threaten a community with the denial of these basic social services if the community failed to support the candidate of the party, although intimidation of an individual voter was itself an offence.

A combination of all these forces progressively eliminated opposition parties in the Regions, and established a virtual one-party system in each. This new pattern began to emerge with the Action Group victory in the West in 1960. It was followed by the landslide victory of the N.P.C. in the North in May 1961, and confirmed by the N.C.N.C. victory in the East in November of the same year. In each case the government exploited to its electoral advantage its control of the administrative machinery to whittle down opposition. And control of the Regional authority ensured for the party possessing it control of the Federal constituencies in that Region. At the 1959 Federal elections, the N.P.C. won 134 of the 178 Federal constituencies in Northern Nigeria and was later joined by 13 successful independent candidates from the West and one from the East. The Action Group won 25 of the Northern constituencies, 34 of the 62 seats in Western Nigeria, 15 of the 73 Eastern seats, and 1 seat from Lagos. Of the 89 seats won by the N.C.N.C., 58 were from constituencies in Eastern Nigeria, 21 from the West, and 8 from the North. At the 1964 federal elections, the N.P.C. won all but 2 of the 172 seats from the North; and the N.C.N.C., all the seats in the East and the Mid-West, where the party was in government. The Action Group, by boycotting the election, won only a handful of seats in the West.

The Action Group Government in the West had been dismissed in May 1962, and after a six-month period of Emergency Administration, a United People's Party (a pro-N.P.C. splinter of the Action Group) Government was installed by the Federal Authority in January 1963. Then, during 1963, the disgruntled

Yoruba members of the N.C.N.C. decided to make common cause with the United People's Party to form a new political grouping in Western Nigeria, under the name of the Nigerian National Democratic Party (N.N.D.P.), with the principal objective of uniting the Yoruba in accommodation with the N.P.C.-dominated Federal Government. Yoruba 'solidarity' and a fair share of the national cake for the Yoruba were chosen as the N.N.D.P. slogans. All the political and economic misfortunes of Western Nigeria in recent years were ascribed to the Action Group's challenge of N.P.C. hegemony. But the Yoruba, the most politically advanced section in Nigeria, were not easily taken in by political slogans, and most refused to join the N.N.D.P., even though it was the party in power. Besides, traditional rivalries and animosities do colour modern party alignments. It is not often that the Ibadan masses will support any movement based on Ijebu leadership, and Ilesha peasants will not usually vote on the same side of the political fence as their old rivals the Ife. Clever political party managers were quick to exploit these traditional rivalries, as well as the slogan of national unity. The general feeling that the N.N.D.P. was the embodiment of insurrection against the established leadership and little more than an N.P.C. satellite prevented it from enjoying mass support. And the more open the support that the N.N.D.P. received from the N.P.C., the closer together it brought the leaders of the N.C.N.C. and their former bitter rivals in the Action Group.

By the middle of 1964, two major political alliances had emerged from all the manoeuvres. The N.P.C. and N.N.D.P. founded the Nigerian National Alliance (N.N.A.) under the leadership of Sir Ahmadu Bello, the Sardauna of Sokoto and Premier of Northern Nigeria; the N.C.N.C. and Action Group constituted themselves into the United Progressive Grand Alliance (U.P.G.A.) under the leadership of Dr M. I. Okpara, Premier of Eastern Nigeria. Both alliances agreed to field joint lists of candidates; and issued manifestos for the Federal parliamentary elections of 30 December 1964.

The period of electioneering was generally one of extravagance, marked by extremes of the trivial and the dangerously hostile. The niceties of the law of defamation were for the duration of the campaign temporarily shelved. Wild accusations marked the platform speeches, and opposing groups accused each other of trying to rig the elections. The festive atmosphere of the ministerial motorcades and their accompanying brass bands and drummers were punctuated with the bloody battles of the private gangs retained by the major political parties. And, at the end of the whole charade, the majority party was confirmed in office, and all political recrimination was put in cold storage until the approach of another election.

The 1964 Federal elections were, however, treated rather more seriously. Every one of the political leaders had publicly stated that he wanted a free and fair election. As an earnest of their desire, indeed, the Prime Minister and the Regional Premiers met early in October to consider what measures should be taken to realize this objective; and three weeks later the Prime Minister convened a conference of all political parties to agree on the appropriate arrangements. All the parties at the conference subscribed to a self-denying ordinance for the maintenance of law and order, agreeing to lift bans on processions and public meetings, facilitate the granting of permits for public meetings and processions, restrain party activists from molesting their political rivals, and generally promote a peaceful atmosphere throughout the election period.

How seriously the party leaders communicated their resolve to their rank and file and their activists is difficult to say, but no party seemed to have abided by the resolution to conduct a free and peaceful campaign. Soon after electioneering started, the minority parties began to complain of obstruction by the party or group of parties in control of the governments of the Regions. Such tactics as inflicting a technical knock-out on the opposition by preventing its candidates from filing their nomination papers within the prescribed time had been commonplace enough. They had been employed by all the majority parties at one time or another against opposition candidates, to secure the unopposed return of a particularly vulnerable party leader who was unpopular in his constituency. But in December 1964 the Publicity Secretary of the N.P.C. indiscreetly boasted to the press before nominations closed that his party would have eighty of its candidates returned unopposed, and in the event the party returned sixty-one candidates unopposed. There followed a flood of protests and anguished cries from the U.P.G.A. leaders that the Nigerian National Alliance (N.N.A.) had not observed any of the terms of agreement reached at the all-party conference; and in a memorandum submitted to the President of the Republic and the Prime Minister (who although a leader of the N.N.A. was acknowledged as an impartial judge), the U.P.G.A. listed the wrongs perpetrated against its candidates and party supporters. The memorandum alleged that U.P.G.A. members and supporters had been arbitrarily arrested and wrongfully imprisoned; and as if that were not enough, that some had been brutally assaulted and in some cases killed. The police had proved totally incompetent and obviously incapable of handling a very serious and highly explosive situation, particularly in Northern Nigeria. The memorandum went on to give specific cases of obstruction, intimidation and undue influence directed against U.P.G.A. candidates and their nominators, and published sworn affidavits from the victims. The complaints listed were the familiar ones made by every minority party at every election; and, no doubt if the N.N.A. had not been so confident of victory, it would have made very similar complaints against the conduct of the U.P.G.A. in Eastern and Mid-Western Nigeria.

The U.P.G.A. leaders appealed for a postponement of the election by the Electoral Commission, but it was clear that neither the Electoral Commission nor even the President was competent to postpone the election without parliamentary sanction. Faced with a situation where at the close of nominations the N.N.A. had won 61 seats unopposed, and violence was steadily increasing, the U.P.G.A. decided to boycott the elections altogether. The decision has since been interpreted by some as a serious tactical blunder and by others as a red herring drawn across the prospect of inevitable defeat and the dismissal of U.P.G.A. Ministers from the Federal Cabinet. But the decision itself precipitated a serious political and constitutional crisis.

According to a State House Diary,[37] released for general information by the Nigerian Federal Ministry of Information on 24 December 1965, a delegation of U.P.G.A. leaders 'conferred with the President of the Republic and warned that unless irregularities which made the Federal Election not free and fair were removed, and the election postponed, they would boycott it.

Dr Okpara threatened that Eastern Nigeria would secede from the Federation.' The President replied that he would be guided by the Constitution. Apparently some of the President's unofficial advisers thought that he had constitutional powers to intervene and postpone the election; for on the same day his Legal Secretary, 'after consultation with several lawyers of repute, advised that since there was conflict of opinion on the powers to be exercised by the President under the Constitution, the Federal Attorney-General should be summoned for official advice.' The following day the President conferred with the Governors of the four Regions, and they 'decided that the Prime Minister should summon a meeting of the Regional Premiers to request them to adhere to their undertaking to conduct a free and fair electioneering campaign.' On 28 December the Prime Minister invited all the Premiers to a conference in Lagos, but none of them agreed to attend. On that same day the President invited the Prime Minister to discuss the situation and suggested to the Prime Minister that, 'in the face of proven irregularities and threats of boycott and secession', the election should be postponed for six months, to enable the United Nations to send experts who would assist in conducting a free and fair election. The Prime Minister rejected the suggestion; and later on the same day the President summoned the Attorney-General (Dr T. O. Elias) for advice on the President's constitutional powers in such circumstances. The Attorney-General advised that the Constitution of the Republic did not confer absolute executive powers on the President and that the President had no power to dismiss the Prime Minister, to assume the powers of Parliament, or appoint an interim or provisional government, as some of the President's official advisers appeared to have suggested to him.

The Attorney-General's advice left it in no doubt that the President had no constitutional power to postpone the election in his absolute discretion, nor could the Federal Electoral Commission lawfully cancel it. The U.P.G.A., therefore, decided to take political action by boycotting the election; and on the eve of polling day, its three nominees in the Electoral Commission resigned. The U.P.G.A. leaders clearly hoped this action would not only embarrass their political opponents, but might reinforce the pressure on the President to declare a state of emergency and set up an interim government. But in spite of the U.P.G.A. decision to boycott the election, polling took place in all the constituencies of Northern and Western Nigeria, where N.N.A. governments were in control, and in Lagos. The Governments of Eastern and Mid-Western Nigeria prohibited polling in their areas of jurisdiction, except in the Warri constituency, where the N.C.N.C. candidate (Chief F. S. Okotie-Eboh, Federal Minister of Finance) defied the prohibition and persuaded polling officers to conduct a poll. The boycott gave the N.N.A. the opportunity to win a landslide victory in both the North and the West, and to win one of the four Lagos seats regarded as safe for the U.P.G.A. Having secured an overwhelming majority, the Prime Minister, who expected to be confirmed in office, called on the President; but he was informed that 'it was not the President's wish to appoint a person to form a government, and that the head of state would rather resign.' The President had decided that, in spite of his Attorney-General's advice to the contrary, the election should not be the basis for a new government, since it had not been conducted in a 'fair and free' atmosphere.

The Chief Justice of the Federation, Sir Adetokunboh Ademola, and the Chief Justice of Eastern Nigeria, Sir Louis Mbanefo, then intervened, and after days of arduous negotiation, the deadlock between the President and his Prime Minister was resolved. A six-point formula, accepted by all the parties, was adopted. The basis of agreement was as follows:

(1) The reaffirmation of the belief in the unity of the Federation of Nigeria, in which every citizen shall have equal opportunity and no one shall be oppressed.

(2) A strict observance of the Constitution until it is amended according to law and the will of the people.

(3) A broad-based national government should be formed on the results of the last election so as to avoid chaos.

(4) The legality of the present election should be determined by the courts and the results of the elections should be upheld, except in certain constituencies where the number of voters was so small as to make a mockery of democracy.

(5) Arrangements should be made within six months to review the constitution and the machinery for election. This should be in the form of a commission of 11, constituted as follows: 1 to be appointed by the President; 2 to be appointed by the Prime

Minister; and 2 by each Regional Premier. The commission should work for one year in order to ascertain the wishes of the people of Nigeria. Then a Constituent Assembly can take the final decision.

(6) Dissolution of the legislature of Western Nigeria, to enable the people of that Region to express their wish as to who should govern them.

The agreement was sealed with the formation of a 'broadly-based' government, by which nearly one-third of the members of the legislature became Ministers or Parliamentary Secretaries. But the wisdom of the decision to form a national government at all did not go unquestioned. There were those who felt that the President should have suspended the Constitution (though he had sworn to uphold it at his inauguration) in order to right the wrongs which they claimed had been inflicted on a section of the community; and there were many who thought that the President, instead of acting as the impartial 'father' of the nation (which he was supposed to be), should have taken up arms with the U.P.G.A. and resisted either the holding of the election on the scheduled date or the acceptance of the results afterwards. Either of these courses of action would have been immediately calamitous for the Federation. The compromise solution gave Nigerian leaders a breathing-space in which to reflect on the defects of their political policies, and provided a basis for further negotiations on constitutional change to reduce the area of friction between the various units of the Federation.

Meanwhile, however, the Federal Authority had been further neutralized by Regional intransigence and tribal solidarity. Politically, the U.P.G.A. boycott had been an error of judgement. The N.C.N.C. had by this political action succeeded in retaining its place in the Federal Cabinet; but it had lost much of its prestige as a national party by threatening the secession of Eastern Nigeria, where it was in absolute control, from the Federation. The capture by the N.N.D.P. of most of the federal parliamentary seats in Western Nigeria by default, and the inclusion of a powerful N.N.D.P. team in the Federal Cabinet, weakened the bargaining position of the N.C.N.C. and gave the N.N.D.P. a fighting chance in Western Nigeria. Had the U.P.G.A., in spite of the odds against it, participated in the election of 30 December, it would have emerged as a very powerful opposition, strengthening the parliamentary system in Nigeria. Instead, by its action, it helped to exacerbate tribal animosities and weakened the prospects of parliamentary democracy in the country. And this was dangerously demonstrated by the many complaints from the minority parties in Eastern and Mid-Western Nigeria that, during the holding of the postponed elections in these areas, the U.P.G.A. employed the same methods against its opponents as had allegedly been employed by the N.N.A. in the Northern and Western Regions earlier in December 1964.

The events of December 1964, serious as they were, paled beside those which followed in Western Nigeria. On 11 October 1965, the people of Western Nigeria went to the polls to elect a Regional Government, the first since the 1962 emergency which had brought the N.N.D.P. into existence. It had for long been evident that, despite its control of the administrative machinery, the N.N.D.P. could not win any genuinely free election against the Action Group opposition in the West. But an Action Group victory in the West would have meant control by the U.P.G.A. of the whole of the South (including Lagos, where the City Council was controlled by the Action Group). Such a political alignment would sooner or later have obliged the N.P.C. to come to terms with the U.P.G.A. and jettison the N.N.D.P., or alternatively would have hastened a North-South showdown in which sizeable areas of the North, including the Middle Belt and Kano Province, might very well have defected from the N.P.C. fold. It was, therefore, crucial to the continuation of N.P.C. hegemony that the N.N.D.P. should win the election and be confirmed in office by the Western electorate. In manipulating the electoral machinery to its advantage, the N.N.D.P. Government of Western Nigeria was merely following a precedent, of course, which all Regional Governments had adopted to perpetuate their rule. In a press statement the Premier, Chief Akintola, pointed out in answer to his critics that in the previous fifteen years no Regional Government had lost an election.[38] On the contrary, at every election since 1956 the government party had increased its majority in the legislature simply because it controlled the electoral machinery; and during the campaigns which preceded the 11 October poll, the Premier and his deputy were alleged to have boasted that 'whether the people voted for them or not, the N.N.D.P. would be returned to power.' But never in the short history of parliamentary elections in Nigeria was there such massive rigging as occurred in Western Nigeria in October.

According to the Chairman of the Federal Electoral Commission, Mr E. E. Esua (the substance of whose statement was not seriously challenged by either the Regional Electoral Commission or the Western Government), there were a number of grave irregularities in the conduct of the election.[39] Many Electoral Officers had, after receiving nominations from the candidates of one party, deserted their posts during the period when they should have been receiving nomination papers from opposing candidates. In some constituencies Electoral Officers were kidnapped after they had received nomination papers from the candidates of one party but before they received papers from candidates of other parties. The appointment of some Electoral Officers was revoked after they had accepted nomination papers from candidates and issued certificates of validity; some of the Electoral Officers appointed in place of those whose appointments had been revoked did not make themselves available to candidates of the opposition parties, and refused to recognize the certificates of validity already issued by their predecessors. As a result, sixteen of the N.N.D.P. candidates were returned unopposed at the close of nominations, even though the U.P.G.A. had paid the election deposit of £100 for each of the ninety-four seats to be contested. U.P.G.A. candidates tried to challenge these unopposed returns in the High Court of Western Nigeria, but were unsuccessful. Section 19(*b*) of the Western Nigeria Electoral Regulations provides that

> if after the latest time for delivery of nomination papers and for the withdrawal of candidates only one person remains validly nominated, that person shall be declared elected;

and Section 14(3) provides that

> the Electoral Officer's decision that the candidate has been validly nominated shall be final and shall not be questioned in any legal proceedings.

Furthermore, there was abundant evidence of the leakage of ballot papers, despite the elaborate security arrangements made by the Electoral Commission for their custody. At several polling stations there was clear 'dumping' of wads of ballot papers; and a number of unauthorized persons, including local government police, were found in unlawful possession of large quantities of ballot papers. Some candidates were declared elected, although scoring a minority of votes; and some candidates who had been declared elected at the counting stations and issued with certificates of election, later found that their defeated opponents were returned by the Electoral Commission as the victors. The most notorious example of this travesty was the case of a man who won the election in one of the Owo constituencies. His opponent was declared the victor. He thereupon announced that he had decided to join the N.N.D.P. A few days after this announcement, the Electoral Commission declared him the successful candidate and quietly dropped his opponent.

Whoever was responsible for these large-scale irregularities, the Nigerian public, and in particular the electorate of Western Nigeria, had no doubt that they enjoyed the sanction of the government of the day. That those who believed that they had been cheated of their right to victory did not avail themselves of the avenues of redress provided by the law, was a serious reflection on our law-enforcing agencies. Nigerians love litigation on political issues. They will fight their opponents in the Courts to the last ditch. During every election, and immediately afterwards, the Courts had been inundated with complaints about non-compliance with some provision or other of the electoral law, and contestants had spent considerable sums of money on election petitions, even though most such petitions had failed after careful judicial scrutiny. But now, for the first time, candidates who had been declared defeated decided not to seek redress in the Courts, and instead took the law into their own hands.

It may well have been true, as the Premier of Western Nigeria claimed, that the wave of lawlessness sweeping the Region after the polls had been excited by the defeated and frustrated U.P.G.A. members.[40] It should, however, be remembered that when the U.P.G.A., through its own political miscalculation, had lost the 1964 Federal election, there had been a spate of election petitions in the Courts. That this time the party should have resorted to self-redress indicated a disease in the Nigerian political system. It was claimed by some people, including so eminent a personage as the Premier of Northern Nigeria, that 'the troubles in the West are being fomented by elements outside the Region.'[41] If this was true, then the Western Government ought seriously to have examined its standing with the people of the Region, whose solidarity and material advantages constituted the N.N.D.P. slogan. There must have been something wrong, if the people so easily succumbed to outside influences.

By Christmas week, disturbances and lawlessness in the West were widespread and still increasing. Indeed, the Nigeria Police virtually admitted that the task of maintaining law and order in many districts of Western Nigeria was beyond them. Nigerian Army troops had to be posted in Ibadan, the Regional capital, and other parts of the Region to enable the Western legislature to meet for just one day. Meanwhile, travellers on some of the highways found themselves at the mercy of thugs who roamed at night molesting innocent and law-abiding citizens. But the Federal authorities refused to intervene because they regarded the situation as one entirely within the competence of the Western Regional Government. The Prime Minister of the Federation was reported to have told a meeting of students at the University of Ibadan that the situation did not warrant the declaration of a state of emergency because, 'even if there were killings, it would still have to be established that there were two Premiers exercising government powers in the region concerned before the Federal Government could step in to declare a state of emergency.'[42] Many people were understandably bewildered as they remembered what had happened in May 1962 when, although there had been no bloodshed, the Federal authority had declared a state of emergency because each of two rival politicians had claimed to be the legally appointed Premier of the Region.

Nigeria was at the brink. Suppression of the opposition by the Regional Government with the backing of both the Federal Government and the Northern Regional Government would provide no lasting solution in Western Nigeria, and would establish the precedent that no Regional Government would ever again allow its opponents to field candidates in any election, a situation which would mark the beginning of dictatorship. Once such a system was allowed to take roots in the Regions, it would be a matter of time before it enveloped the whole of Nigeria. The country had had enough pointers to the possible patterns of power distribution. What happened in Western Nigeria in 1962 showed that as long as Northern Nigeria was under the overwhelming political domination of one party, it was possible for that party, by allying itself with one or the other of the other regionally-based parties, to dictate the tempo and direction of power politics in Nigeria. In 1962, the N.C.N.C., by allying itself with the N.P.C., assisted in incarcerating the Action Group. Now the N.N.D.P. was itching for an opportunity to humiliate the N.C.N.C. The dangers of extreme regionalism, anchored in tribalism, were more apparent now than they had ever been before.

To condemn tribalism is not to decry the concept of tribe. It is a natural phenomenon in human social organization that some people should claim descent from a common ancestor. The group of people who claim such descent may be small or large. It is purely an accident that one is born into any of these groups. In small-scale societies, membership of any of these groups confers certain benefits and reciprocal obligations; but as the scale of social organization increases, these rights and obligations, as they become irrelevant, gradually disappear, some naturally, others by deliberate effort. The population of Nigeria comprises many such social groups or tribes. We are all familiar with the argument that Nigeria is a mere geographical expression, brought into existence by the fiat of the British Government. This is an old argument, and Bernard Shaw put it neatly in *St Joan*, where one of the characters, the Earl of Warwick, says to the Chaplain De Stogumber:

> A Frenchman! Where did you pick up that expression? Are these Burgundians and Bretons and Picards and Gascons beginning to call themselves Frenchmen, just as our fellows are beginning to call themselves Englishmen? They actually talk of France and England as their countries. Theirs, if you please! What is to become of me and you if that way of thinking comes into fashion?

In the colonial days, when the so-called detribalized Nigerians referred to themselves as Nigerians, British colonial Earl

Warwicks asked the same question: Are these Ibos and Yorubas and Kanuris, Edos and Ibibios beginning to call themselves Nigerians? Of course Nigeria consists of Ibos and Yorubas and Hausas, and hundreds of other distinct cultural groups; but England consists of Angles and Picts, and Normans and Celts, yet England is a nation, and Russia and America are nations. Indeed every one of the great nations of today started as a mere geographical expression, and in time built up from the different ethnic and cultural elements within its boundaries a cultural complex that today gives it its peculiar national character. No nation is completely homogeneous, either in its racial composition or in its cultural background. When Nigerians were struggling to become politically independent, they did not remember to fight as Ibos, or Yorubas, separate cultural groups; but now that independence has been achieved, the lust for power and personal aggrandizement has revived the myth of tribal exclusiveness. Tribal exclusiveness is a myth because no one tribe is completely different from all others.

Tribal sentiment has, indeed, many practical accomplishments to its credit. 'Tribal Improvement Unions' have been the torch-bearers of progress in many parts of the country. They have provided many of the leading professionals of today. They have been the pioneers in the movement for self-help, which has enabled Nigeria to provide for its people many of the basic social amenities which they now enjoy. To the extent that tribalism proclaims the doctrine of 'I am my brother's keeper' it has been an instrument for good; but a tribe is as much a political unit as a cultural one, and when it acts in the context of modern representative government as a source of political allegiance, then inevitably it comes into conflict with the concept of nationhood. Modern political parties should be based on social and economic ideologies which cut across tribal groupings. When, therefore, a 'Tribal Improvement Union' uses its influence to select a candidate for a constituency and ensure his victory at the polls, it is retarding nationhood in Nigeria. The problem for Nigerian politicians is that, while they sincerely believe in nationwide political parties based on social and economic ideologies, they feel obliged to appeal to tribal loyalties every time their political position is threatened by their rivals.

An equally divisive factor is religion, though there are no political parties organized on a religious basis. Attempts have, indeed, been made at various times to establish a Moslem party in Western Nigeria and a Catholic party in Eastern Nigeria, but they have met with no success. Yet the N.P.C., while not a Moslem party, is supported by the overwhelming majority of Moslems in the North, and since Islam in the North has many strong affinities with Islam in many countries of the Middle East, Nigeria's foreign policy has been ambivalent. External relations were within the exclusive jurisdiction of the Federal Government. And the Federal Government of Nigeria, in accordance with its declared policy of non-alignment, maintained diplomatic relations with both Israel and the Arab countries. The Government of Northern Nigeria, however, did not recognize the existence of Israel, even though Northern Nigeria was an integral part of the Federation. There has been religious tolerance in Nigeria, and so no Nigerian Government has interfered with conscientious objections based on religious persuasion; but religious differences did mean that the Northern Regional Government had a foreign policy inconsistent with overall Nigerian foreign policy in significant respects. To tolerate the existence of a state within a state – on whatever grounds – cannot but impede the development of true nationhood.

The dangers of those factors which limit the full attainment of nationhood must, however, be put in proper perspective against the gathering momentum of the centripetal forces. There can be no doubt that national cohesion will endure. Regional intransigence may succeed in impeding the progress towards full nationhood for some time, but the state will not disintegrate. The threat of secession is not new to Nigerians. When in 1953 the present leaders of the N.P.C. feared political and economic domination of the North by the South, they threatened secession. A few years later, the Action Group, faced with the combined opposition of the East and North, and believing that the political influence of the West fell far short of its economic contribution to the prosperity of the Federation, threatened secession. In 1965 the leaders of Eastern Nigeria, finding that, despite the now favourable economic position of the Region, their political influence was weakened by the N.P.C./N.N.D.P. alliance, threatened secession.

The threat of secession is a convenient emotional expression of political frustration. But no Regional leader seriously believes that it is a practical alternative to Nigeria's problem of adjustment to the modern world. Indeed, no Region of the Federation can afford to go it alone. The East, in spite of growing riches from oil, would be faced with an unprecedented employment problem if it broke away from the rest of the country. There are at least one million Ibo of Eastern Nigerian origin resident in other parts of the Federation, and if the East seceded, most of these would be forced to return there. The present political leaders of Eastern Nigeria are too realistic to contemplate such an event with equanimity; besides, the East is not linguistically homogeneous. The non-Ibo communities in the Region would oppose secession to the point of breaking away from an independent Eastern Nigeria. And what is true of the East is true too of the North where, in addition to the dominant Hausa-Fulani linguistic group, there are several non-Hausa groups like the Tiv, the Birom and Yoruba who would passionately oppose the establishment of a separate Northern Nigeria, politically linked to the Arab world. On economic grounds alone, if on no other, the West and the North could ill afford to secede. Indeed, the economies of the various Regions are so complementary to each other that no severe fluctuation in the export price of one Region's main primary product has ever produced violent fluctuations in the economy as a whole. For instance, the present low price of cocoa, the main export crop of Western Nigeria, in the world market has not caused any substantial fall in the public revenues of the Federation as a whole or of Western Nigeria in particular, because of the diversified pattern of the country's export crop production, which is taken into account in the system of revenue allocation. Nigeria's linguistic heterogeneity and diversified economy militate against secession while they favour closer union and central direction.

Nigerians in all walks of life, irrespective of their political affiliation and tribal connexion, have come to appreciate the significance in international affairs of their country's size, even though most of them are not yet able to transfer their loyalty from their tribe. They have taken pride in their national representatives whenever they have performed well at international conferences. The peace-keeping role of Nigerian troops in the Congo and Tanzania gave general satisfaction to the masses of Nigerians who wanted to see their country give positive leadership to Africa. The part played by Nigeria in the expulsion of South Africa from the Commonwealth and her conciliation of the opposing factions in the Organization of African Unity were all applauded by the masses of the people. Equally, any act of the Federal Government which appeared to detract from Nigeria's leadership role or her national sovereignty was loudly condemned. The Anglo-Nigerian Defence Agreement had to be abrogated because it was regarded as a commitment detracting from Nigeria's sovereignty.

The present generation of political leaders is doing precious little to nurture a national attachment; but other forces are at work. Nigerian students and intellectuals, though organizationally weak at present, are talking and writing about national unity and loyalty to Nigeria rather than to any tribe or region. The Nigerian Army has shown on every occasion that it has been required to restore law and order that it is truly Nigerian, impartial and disciplined. During the 1965 disorders in Western Nigeria, the Army proved to be the sole completely impartial body in the discharge of the duty assigned to it. All these gathering forces point to the conclusion that Nigeria is unlikely to disintegrate even under the powerful centrifugal forces of tribalism.

9. The Army Intervenes

At midnight on Sunday 16 January 1966, Nigeria's First Republic came to an abrupt end. A few minutes earlier, the Acting President of the Republic, Dr Nwafor Orizu, had announced in a radio broadcast that the Council of Ministers had voluntarily and unanimously decided to hand over the government of the Federation to the armed forces, 'in view of the present situation in the country'. Immediately after the Acting President's announcement, the General Officer Commanding the Nigerian Army, Major-General J. T. Aguiyi-Ironsi, accepted the invitation on behalf of the armed forces, and announced that he had been invested with authority as Head of the Federal Military Government and Supreme Commander of the Armed Forces. He issued a decree forthwith suspending those sections of the Nigerian Constitution which provided for the offices of President, Prime Minister, and Parliament; and for Regional Governors, Premiers, Executive Councils and Regional Legislatures. He directed that:

> there shall be a Military Governor in each of the existing four Regions; but the last holder of the Office of Governor in each Region will hold the office of Adviser to the Military Governor of the Region. The Chief Justice and all other Judges shall continue to hold office, and the judiciary shall continue to function normally under the present Statute . . . All Civil Servants, the Nigeria Police Force and the special Constabulary Force shall continue to function as at present; but all local government and Native Authority police shall henceforth be under the control of the Inspector-General of Police.

He announced that it was the intention of the Military Government to stamp out the disorder in Western Nigeria and in the Tiv Division of Northern Nigeria, and to maintain law and order until a constitution acceptable to the people had been worked out. The new administration, he said, would honour all international agreements and financial obligations entered into by the previous government.

The day before, the Council of Ministers had issued the following statement:

> In the early hours of this morning, 15 January 1966, a dissident section of the Nigerian Army kidnapped the Prime Minister and the Minister of Finance and took them to an unknown destination. The General Officer Commanding the Nigerian Army and the vast majority of the Nigerian Army remain completely loyal to the Federal Government and are already taking all appropriate measures to bring the situation under control. All essential public services continue to function normally. The Federal Government is satisfied that the situation will soon return to normal and that the ill-advised mutiny will be brought to an end, and that law and order in the few disturbed areas of the country will soon be restored. All public buildings and establishments in the Federal Territory are being guarded by loyal troops.

The 'ill-advised mutiny' occurred simultaneously in Lagos, Enugu, Kano, Ibadan and Kaduna; in the last two Regional capitals, the official residences of the Regional Premiers were attacked, and the two Premiers, with some of their guards, killed. By nightfall on the same day the 'mutineers' were in control of Kaduna and Ibadan. Enugu appeared to have come under the control of 'loyal' troops quite early in the day and so escaped damage and bloodshed. By the Sunday morning one of the leaders of the revolt, a Major Chukuma Nzeogwu, had assumed administrative control of Northern Nigeria and announced that he had appointed a government of civil servants for the Region 'to stamp out tribalism, nepotism and regionalism'. He appealed to all to cooperate with the new régime so as to establish 'a free country, devoid of corruption, nepotism, tribalism and regionalism'. This was the first public indication by the leaders of the military coup of the objectives of the 'mutiny'. And with the announcement of these objectives, the coup was immediately hailed by many Nigerians as a rescue of the country from disaster.

To appreciate the relief with which so many Nigerians greeted the coup, one must look at the course of events during the fortnight immediately preceding the 'mutiny'. The violence and political thuggery provoked by the results of the October Regional election in Western Nigeria were daily growing in intensity and extent. It was becoming increasingly clear to many enlightened Nigerians that the Prime Minister's reluctance to intervene publicly to bring about a compromise settlement of the crisis in the West was the result of political pressure from the leader of his party, the Sardauna of Sokoto, Premier of the North. Many outstanding persons of Western origin had, with the Prime Minister's personal approval, made strenuous efforts throughout December to find a solution, but the leaders of the N.N.D.P. refused to consider any compromise, let alone agree to an all-party government for the West which would pave the way for fresh elections before the end of the statutory five-year period of the newly elected legislature.* The Prime Minister was known to favour just this compromise proposal, and many non-partisan Nigerians, familiar with the practice of settling political disagreements of this kind by negotiation, publicly expressed apprehension about the Northern Premier's political objectives. It appeared to many that Western Nigeria was being used as a political pawn in some grand design. And so many who had hitherto remained neutral felt constrained openly to support the U.P.G.A. protest.

Because it was widely believed that the Prime Minister's careful efforts to promote Commonwealth unity of purpose on the Rhodesian issue was a political device to divert attention from the deteriorating situation in Western Nigeria, the violence in the West and the suburbs of Lagos was intensified on the eve of the Commonwealth Conference, so that despite the vigilance of the police, it became increasingly difficult to travel through many parts of the Region. There were widespread cases of robbery, murder, arson and attacks on police patrols. When, therefore, the Federal Parliament was summoned for 12 January 1966, many members who had themselves been victims of the violence hoped that the situation in Western Nigeria would be discussed. But

* At the interview which the late Prime Minister granted to the correspondent of the weekly *West Africa,* he clearly put the blame for the continuation of the troubles in Western Nigeria on the N.N.D.P. which refused to consider the possibility of an all-party Government for Western Nigeria and fresh elections before the statutory five-year period of the legislature expired. The Prime Minister preferred conciliation to the use of force for settling the Western Nigeria political crisis. He was, however, overruled in this by his party leader, Sir Ahmadu Bello.

when the matter was raised in the House of Representatives on 13 January, the Parliamentary Secretary to the Prime Minister announced that the Federal Government regarded the disturbances in Western Nigeria as the responsibility of the Regional Government. It was officially admitted that some 153 persons had lost their lives in these disturbances, although unofficial reports put the estimates at many times that figure. The crisis was then further inflamed by reports that the Premier of Western Nigeria, as leader of the N.N.D.P., had visited Kaduna on 14 January to consult Sir Ahmadu Bello, the leader of the N.N.A., on what action should be taken to stamp out the disturbances. There was general apprehension that extreme measures were being prepared by the Western Nigeria authorities, with the backing of the Northern Government, against leaders of the U.P.G.A. in Western Nigeria and other parts of the Federation.

It was in this explosive situation, when the Government of Western Nigeria had lost the power to govern and the Federal Government itself seemed unwilling to exercise its overall responsibility for the maintenance of law and order, that certain army officers attempted to seize control. Their revolt was widespread, well coordinated and effective. According to the leading figure of the revolt, Major Chukuma Nzeogwu, the mutineers constituted a national company.

> Most of those concerned with the revolt in the North were Northerners. All the officers and men who took part in the coup received no personal rewards. They did it for the good of the country. This is why we have gone out of our way to avoid bloodshed. We are anxious for peace.

Having achieved this remarkable success, the mutineers surrendered meekly to the General Officer Commanding the Nigerian Army, and declared their loyalty to him as Supreme Commander and Head of the Federal Military Government.

Well might the men who planned and executed the coup be satisfied, for the Army take-over was hailed by every section of the country, including the political parties in power at the time of the coup. Within three days of the establishment of the military government, the N.P.C., the dominant party in the broad-based Federal Government, announced that 'the party regards the transfer of authority as the only solution to the many recent problems facing the country', and after calling on all its supporters to cooperate with the military administration in bringing peace and stability to Nigeria, expressed the party's belief that 'the paramount task of the military régime is the welfare of the peoples of Nigeria, irrespective of tribal origin or political persuasion.' The N.N.D.P., the party ousted from power in Western Nigeria, also welcomed the military take-over and assured the new government of its 'full cooperation in the arduous task of building a prosperous and unified Nigeria', while its Youth Wing called for 'an end to bribery, corruption, nepotism and tribalism'. The N.C.N.C. and its ally, the Action Group, expressed support for the new régime in similarly clear terms. Both parties said that they saw in the army take-over a continuation of the people's struggle to preserve parliamentary democracy, the rule of law, respect for human dignity and the unity of the federation. Chiefs, trade union officials and Church leaders welcomed the army take-over just as much as the masses of the people seemed to do.

Nigeria came under the rule of a military government which comprised a Supreme Military Council and a Federal Executive Council, both of them headed by Major-General Aguiyi-Ironsi. Membership of the Supreme Military Council included the Heads of the Nigerian Navy and Air Force, the Army Chief of Staff, and the four Military Governors who took charge of the former Regions, now termed Provinces. Membership of the Federal Executive Council included the members of the Supreme Military Council together with the Inspector-General of Police, his Deputy, and the Attorney-General of the Federation. The Federal Executive Council performed the functions of the former Council of Ministers. In the Provinces there were Executive Councils presided over by the respective Military Governors and including the Commissioner of Police, the Chief Law Officer, and top civil servants. The Military Governors were themselves directly responsible to the Head of the Federal Military Government and Supreme Commander.

The military government began its rule with the suspension of some sections of the Nigerian Constitution and with the dissolution of all political parties in the country. It made a strong bid for popular support. Within two days of its taking office, it began dismantling some of the most ruinous measures taken by the previous administration. One of the first of these (and perhaps one of the most important) to be scrapped was the ban that had been placed on certain newspapers by local government councils with the connivance of the Regional Governments. This had followed a complaint by the Leader of the N.C.N.C., Dr Michael Okpara, that some Nigerian newspapers had failed to discharge their public duty in not condemning with sufficient vigour the irregularities committed during the fateful Western Nigeria election. Soon after Dr Okpara's public criticism, the Onitsha Urban County Council in Eastern Nigeria had imposed a ban on the circulation of certain Nigerian newspapers (the *Daily Times*, *Morning Post* and *Daily Sketch*) within its area of jurisdiction, and this ban had then been adopted by the Enugu City Council and a number of other important local government bodies in Eastern Nigeria. Because Onitsha, Enugu and Port Harcourt are the principal points of entry into Eastern Nigeria for newspapers published outside the Region, the ban had accordingly deprived Eastern Nigeria residents of their fundamental right to choose what newspapers they wanted to read, in clear breach of Section 24 of the Nigerian Constitution, which enshrined the right to 'freedom of expression, including freedom to hold opinions and to receive and impart ideas and information without interference'. And this infringement of individual rights had been committed by minor governmental authorities with impunity on the pretext that their councils were protesting against the rigging of an election in another part of the Federation. Indeed so self-righteous had the petty local government despots become that the mildest protest from a university professor in Eastern Nigeria had been loudly condemned by the Eastern Nigeria Government-owned newspaper, the *Nigerian Outlook*, as an act of sabotage against the people. The Ibadan City Council had then taken reprisal measures by banning the circulation of the *West African Pilot* and the *Nigerian Tribune*, both of which supported the U.P.G.A. cause, and later the *Daily Times* for publishing reports which were unfavourable to the N.N.D.P. government. That in spite of the protests from newspaper owners and readers, no government in the country had taken steps to order the withdrawal of the ban, illustrates the degree to which political passions had deprived the governments of their sense of duty to the people who had put them in office.

To deprive people of the right to choose what books to read is a serious infringement of individual liberty, even in a community less than half of whose members are literate in any language. It is almost a deprivation of life to deny them the right of access to pipe-borne water on political grounds; and yet some communities had suffered just such deprivation. In Western Nigeria, though water-supply undertakings had been completed many months before the fateful election, they had not been put into service because the party in power wanted the supply of water to be used as an election bait, and the government had decided to withhold the release of the water until it knew which way the communities concerned would vote; in Eastern Nigeria the water supply to some villages had been turned off on the instructions of the Regional Government because their inhabitants had persistently refused to vote for the candidate of the government party at every election. The military government on assumption of office ordered the immediate release of water to these communities.

These are only a few of the many strange measures – some crude, others more subtle – by which all Regional Governments perpetuated themselves in office and, by implication, determined the colour of the Federal Government. Such measures were not motivated merely by tribal animosities. In the two examples given above, the victims of the tyranny were communities belonging to the same cultural group as the majority party in the respective Regions. The measures were, rather, calculated to stifle political opposition to the party in power. Tribalism has certainly been the ladder by which many Nigerian political leaders have climbed to power; but once they have reached the top, they have treated with the same ruthlessness all opposition, whether from members of their own cultural group or not. The use of political power is, indeed, one of the basic problems which Nigeria, like most newly independent countries, finds difficult to solve. The military régime in Nigeria itself saw the problem in terms of extreme sectionalism and corruption. The Head of the Federal Military Government urged, therefore, that 'tribal loyalties and activities which promote tribal consciousness and sectional interests must give way to the urgent task of reconstruction'; and he promised that 'the Federal Military Government will stamp out corruption and dishonesty in our public life with ruthless efficiency, and restore integrity and self-respect in our public life.'

The military government proceeded to take several measures designed to convince the masses that it meant to pursue this policy to its logical conclusion. Political appointees were removed from membership of public boards and statutory corporations, and the number of Ministries was reduced; it is estimated that some £3 million a year were saved for the Nigerian taxpayer by the abolition of these political offices. In addition, politically-coloured Scholarship Boards were disbanded. Customary Courts (one of the principal weapons of political blackmail) were deprived of their criminal jurisdiction, while many local government councils and their Tax Assessment Committees were dissolved. Political parties were banned, and increasing numbers of former political office-holders were detained 'in the interest of state security' or charged in Court for offences ranging from fraud to abuse of office. That within two months of the army take-over, thirty-two top politicians were imprisoned for offences involving moral turpitude suggests the reckless disregard for normal standards of integrity which characterized the conduct of public affairs in the First Republic. But popular though these measures seemed to be, they were in essence therapeutic and negative; the success of the military régime required positive social and economic policies.

In the social and economic areas, several popular measures were, indeed, taken. Soon after the army assumption of power, the price of petrol was cut by 2½d a gallon, and this, with some of the other measures announced, was moderately effective in reducing food prices throughout much of the country. A housing programme for the lower-income groups was launched in Lagos, and similar projects were promised for the provinces. Considerably more attention was given than ever before to the welfare of Moslems who undertook the annual pilgrimage to Mecca. These were popular measures designed to restore the confidence of the ordinary man in government.

More significantly, the Head of the Federal Military Government promised at the beginning of his tenure of office that administrative reforms would be introduced in order to lay a solid foundation for the concept of 'One Nigeria'. Matters which were formerly within the legislative competence of the Regions would be reviewed to facilitate central direction and control over 'issues of national importance and uniform development' in the social and economic fields. Educational policy would be recast and made more directly related to the manpower needs of Nigeria and the problem of unemployment among young school leavers. Government commercial and industrial development policy would be reassessed so that priority would be given to those projects which would rapidly accelerate economic growth; for instance, the iron and steel project would be started without delay. As a first step towards these objectives, the Head of the Federal Military Government appointed a number of study groups to examine the problems involved in refashioning public policies and programmes to meet the new emphasis on national unity, and to submit proposals on constitutional changes, administrative and institutional rearrangements, in the context of the popular wish for centralism. There were working parties to examine such subjects as the administration of justice, and the reorganization of the public services, statutory corporations and state-owned commercial undertakings, educational services and government information media. There was a study group tackling the problems of national economic planning, and another considering proposals for a new Constitution. The last group was expected to produce a working paper which would form the basis of a constitutional review by a Constituent Assembly, and the Head of the Military Government announced that whatever proposals were adopted by a Constituent Assembly would be the subject of a referendum by the people.

Quite naturally, the subject of constitutional review attracted more attention than any of the other measures announced by the government. A great debate swept the Nigerian press, the universities, the clubs and the Churches on what type of constitution should be adopted for the Second Republic. The action of the military government itself indicated the direction in which it would want to see the country move constitutionally. The term 'Region' was replaced by 'Province'; the offices of the Agents-General, who represented the former Regional Governments, were abolished, and their functions transferred to the Office of the Nigerian High Commissioner in London. More and more senior civil servants from the Regional administrations were transferred to Lagos to carry out special duties. Apparently the military government believed that the popular will was for greater centralization or a reversion to a unitary form of government. Certainly, popular opinion in Lagos and most of the urban centres in the South clearly favoured the return to unitary government. The character of popular opinion in the North was much less clear, beyond the overwhelming expression of view that Nigeria should not return to the politics of the First Republic.

It was not unnatural that most Nigerians should be looking for a cure for the diseases of the First Republic in a new constitution. The Republican Constitution (which was basically the 1954 Constitution trimmed to fit an independent country) was a charter for Regional obscurantism. The 1954 Constitution aimed at the establishment of three separate and distinct territories. It was the lowest common denominator between those who wanted three Nigerias, linked by a central agency or common services organization, and those who wanted one Nigeria, with a 'strong centre' exercising exclusive legislative functions in many fields and residual powers in all. The defects of that constitution accounted for many of the difficulties and troubles of the last three years, but not for all of them. Whatever else may be laid at its door, it was not responsible for the widespread corruption and nepotism which marked the career of the First Republic. On the contrary, the Preamble to the Republican Constitution set out in general terms the fundamental moral and political principles upon which the Nigerian nation was conceived.

> Having firmly resolved to establish the Federal Republic of Nigeria, with a view to ensuring the unity of our people and faith in our fatherland, for the purpose of promoting inter-African cooperation and solidarity, in order to assure world peace and international understanding, and so as to further the ends of liberty, equality and justice both in our country and in the world at large, we the people of Nigeria, by our representatives here in Parliament assembled, do hereby declare, enact and give to ourselves the following Constitution.

This preamble reads more like an election manifesto than a legal document; but the principles it set forth, although incapable of direct legal enforcement, are so fundamentally sound that they should at all times form the basis of any new constitution for Nigeria. The question to which Nigerians should address themselves ought not to be simply whether to adopt a unitary or federal constitution, but rather what form of constitutional arrangement would in the circumstances of today facilitate the achievement of the basic principles set forth in the preamble to the Republican Constitution – 'ensuring the unity of our people' and furthering the ends of 'liberty, equality and justice both in our country and in the world at large'.

The 1954 Constitution gave secondary emphasis to the principles of 'liberty, equality and justice'. The problem which preoccupied the makers of that constitution was that of 'unity in diversity', with the emphasis on 'diversity'. The popular cliché then became 'national unity', with the emphasis on 'unity', while the fundamental principles of 'liberty, equality and justice' were apparently taken for granted. What Nigeria needs is a constitution which will promote 'unity' on the basis of individual liberty, equality before the law, and justice for all. This means that in drafting a new constitution, Nigerians should look back at the old constitution and determine for themselves those defects in it which prevented the promotion of 'individual liberty, equality before the law, and justice for all'.

Some of the measures taken by the military government plainly promoted administrative centralism. For example, the Head of the Military Government appointed all Supreme Court and High Court Judges on the advice of a Judicial Advisory Council, which consisted of all the Chief Justices under the Chairmanship of the Chief Justice of the Supreme Court. The Federal Attorney-General was empowered to initiate prosecutions in any part of the Federation, and the annual budgets of the various administrations were to be considered together in one document and approved by the Federal Military Council. Every effort was made to achieve closer integration of the component units of the Federation.

It is, indeed, essential that in framing the next constitution, some basic political principles should be clearly established; and in doing this, we should constantly refer to the experience of the past. The most serious charge ever made against the last Federal

Government, by its opponents and supporters alike, was that from 1964 it lost the will to govern. There was considerable justification for this charge; but there were a number of extenuating circumstances, not the least of which were the constitutional limitations imposed upon the Federal authority in the exercise of its powers, and the concentration of personal political power outside the Federal Cabinet. The late Prime Minister, Sir Abubakar Tafawa Balewa, was by common consent one of the strongest advocates of Nigerian unity; but his domestic policies were singularly unsuccessful, because most of his efforts in this sphere were spent on reconciling the widely divergent views of his Regionalist colleagues, with the result that he lost the initiative for positive leadership.

The first consideration in formulating a new constitution should be the overriding need for a government that will have the power to govern. The power to govern broadly denotes the power (*a*) to control the defence of the entire population of Nigeria and its territory, and to preserve the public peace against all attack, whether from within or from without; (*b*) to regulate trade both within Nigeria and between Nigeria and other countries; (*c*) to control the external relations between all sections of Nigeria and other countries; and (*d*) to ensure a common standard of social justice for all Nigerians, irrespective of ethnic origins, religious beliefs, political persuasion and economic circumstances. These powers ought to be invested in the general government without the slightest constitutional limitation, because it is impossible to foresee all the differing circumstances in which it may be expedient to invoke any or a combination of these powers in the interest of the community. To illustrate the argument we may refer to one of the express powers invested in governments by the previous constitution, the power to maintain law and order. The constitution imposed upon both the Federal and Regional authorities the duty to maintain law and order within their respective areas of jurisdiction, but then proceeded to fetter the power of the Federal authority to perform this duty by limiting the circumstances in which it might intervene in intra-Regional disturbances to maintain law and order. The effect of that constitutional provision was to place a heavy responsibility upon the Federal authority without the corresponding power to discharge it, and conversely to invest the Regional authorities with considerable power and little or no responsibility. The world has seen in the recent Western Nigeria crisis an example of how such power without responsibility could be exploited by a chauvinistic Regional authority. It has been argued, with considerable justification, that in spite of the constitutional limitation placed upon the Federal authority in the exercise of its duty to maintain law and order throughout the Federation, the Federal Government could have intervened without declaring a state of emergency to restore peace in Western Nigeria. We must, however, submit that the exercise by the Federal Government of any executive function normally exerciseable by a Regional Government without declaring a state of emergency would have been politically objectionable. It is, therefore, essential that in any future constitution the duty to maintain law and order and the power to discharge that duty should be vested in one and the same authority.

A short while before the military coup of January 1966, the then Premier of Northern Nigeria shocked many Nigerian journalists by declaring that, for him, the State of Israel did not exist. In other words the Government of Northern Nigeria did not recognize the legal government of Israel. Many Nigerians considered this statement an affront to the Federal Government, which under Schedule I of the Independence Constitution had exclusive jurisdiction over external affairs. A closer examination of the powers of the Federal authority in respect of external affairs, however, reveals that they were in fact not exclusive. Section 69 of the Constitution provides that:

> Parliament may make laws for Nigeria or any part thereof with respect to matters not included in the Legislative Lists for the purpose of implementing any treaty, convention or agreement between the Federation and any other country or any arrangement with or decision of an international organization of which the Federation is a member: Provided that any provision of law enacted in pursuance of this section shall not come into operation in a Region unless the Governor of that Region has consented to its having effect.

This simply meant that in such matters as education (other than higher education), agriculture, health and other residual matters, the Federal executive authority could not legislate to implement international agreements without the express approval of the

Regional Governments. In respect of any such matter, notwithstanding the constitutional provision that external affairs were the exclusive responsibility of the Federal authority, a Regional Government might refuse to give its consent or approval to legislation enacted by the Federal legislature. If, therefore, the Federal Government entered into an agreement with the Government of Israel to supply scientific apparatus to all secondary schools in Nigeria, the Government of Northern Nigeria could, exercising its constitutional right, quite properly have refused to allow the use of such scientific apparatus in any secondary school in Northern Nigeria. No Nigerian need have been surprised that the Northern Region Premier was pursuing a different foreign policy from that of the Federal Government.

Constitutional limitations on federal power abounded in all spheres of government action, and the effect of all such limitations was that the accident of birth or residence in one Region or another determined the measure of social services, the degree of personal freedom, and the standard of living enjoyed by different groups of Nigerian citizens. These basic differences between Nigerians can be removed by constitutional measures. The simplest solution appears to be the establishment of a single legislative body for the whole country. If this proposition is accepted, the next consideration should be the physical problems posed by the sheer size of the country, the inadequate system of communications, and the low level of literacy. These make administrative devolution inescapable. Administration of Maiduguri or Ogoja from a central ministry in Lagos may be desirable in principle, but it presents many practical difficulties. It is, therefore, necessary to devolve some executive powers to smaller units of administration at several critical points away from Lagos. The main question must be the optimum size of the administrative unit, and the answer will in turn depend upon the functions which this unit ought to discharge. If we accept the principle of one supreme law-making body for all Nigeria, then the fewer the legislative functions exercised by other units of government, the less friction there will be between them and the central authority. The terms 'Central' and 'Provincial' Government were reintroduced by the military authorities to express the idea of a single superior and a number of subordinate governments; but the existing provinces were co-terminous with the former Regions. Any constitutional change should, therefore, involve the division of the former Regions into smaller administrative units.

These units should exercise original legislative authority, if any, only in the fields of primary and secondary education, agriculture, health, traditional marriage systems and succession under these systems, and with the proviso that legislation passed by provisional authorities should be subject to the approval of the Central authority. Provincial authorities should also be vested with wide powers of delegated legislation and the maximum administrative control that is practicable over their domestic affairs, subject again to the ultimate authority of the Central administration. If the legislative functions of the Provincial Governments are thus limited to the spheres mentioned above, then the number of provinces can be anything between nine and fifteen, according to the wishes of the people. If the people of Nigeria can find a satisfactory practical solution to the problem of relating the function and size of the unit of government on the one hand, and the optimum distribution of executive authority between the Central Government and the unit government on the other, then the prospects for national integration of the various cultural groups into one Nigerian nation should be good.

Constitutional provisions in themselves, however, invaluable though they may be, have a limited practical effect in facilitating national integration. A great deal depends upon the men who work the constitution. Provisions may be inserted in the constitution to prevent tribalism or nepotism, abuse of office or corruption; but without a core of people dedicated to the task of upholding the principles of the constitution and setting and maintaining a high standard of integrity in public life, constitutional provisions will be violated with impunity, as indeed they were recently. No set of electoral laws can completely prevent the 'rigging' of elections, unless both the people who administer the laws and those for whom they are made submit to them. There can be no complete legal or administrative insurance against the misappropriation of public funds, unless the trustees of these funds as well as the public at large literally regard them as their own money, not that of an alien government. Nigerians at large have to develop a wider view of their area of social responsibility for corporate rights and duties, an area which must transcend the family, clan, tribe or region, and encompass the whole nation. This wider view of social responsibility will require a considerable amount of public educational effort by the present small Nigerian elite, comprising the five per cent of the population who by virtue of education and training carry the burden of administering the country, whether in government, the Church, education, commerce or industry. These people's conception of a nation is different from that of the other ninety-five per cent of the country.

The five per cent 'elite' who conceive of Nigeria as an international personality have a duty: first, to maintain the integrity of that personality; and next, to educate the mass of their compatriots to uphold the integrity of the nation. They have the duty to promote functional interdependence between the different groups in the country; to set the norms of public conduct; and to evolve an ideology which will bind the nation together.

Nigeria cannot return to the old pattern of political organization. A Northern People's Congress based on religious solidarity or a National Convention of Nigerian Citizens founded on appeal to tribal loyalty would be a negation of the principles upon which the Second Republic should be built. Therefore, although the military régime's avowed aim is to hand back power to a civilian government as soon as the wrongs of the past have been righted and a constitution acceptable to the people has been worked out, there will be no properly organized political party to hand over to for some time to come. Quite apart from the ban placed on political activities, the remnants of the old political parties, with their sources of finance now cut off, cannot establish any effective machinery to conduct an election campaign on a nation-wide basis. A sudden return to representative government now would produce a legislature of individuals with no organized programme for running a government. The indications are that the rule of the military will have to continue for a few years, and this prospect does not at present raise any apprehensions in the minds of people whose disgust with the politicians is still very strong. The measures so far taken by the military government have been popular; but the government has yet to face the major problem of the country, which is the menacing increase in the numbers of unemployed school leavers.

It has already been pointed out that following the introduction of universal primary education, some 400,000 pupils complete primary education every year, not more than ten per cent of whom enter secondary schools and other types of post-primary institutions. The overwhelming majority of the remainder enter the labour market. In its present state, the Nigerian economy cannot absorb all these school leavers. On the other hand, primary education is imposing an increasingly crippling burden on resources, with the result that money which could have been effectively used to train the technicians and craftsmen so vital to the faster development of the economy is swallowed up by the rising cost of primary education. The politicians of the previous régime, harrassed though they were by the conflicting results of the policy of universal primary education, dared not abandon it on grounds of political expedience. The military régime is not plagued by such political considerations. It can, therefore, take a more rational attitude to the problem. The immediate task before the government will be to increase employment opportunities for the young school leavers; to provide technical training for as many of them as possible, and disciplined training for some. The long-term solution of the problem must, however, lie in a reappraisal of the country's whole educational policy. It may well be necessary to reallocate public financial resources between the different categories of education. Nigerian parents appreciate the social value of education and are willing to make sacrifices in order that their children may acquire it. It will, therefore, be a more efficient use of resources to transfer the burden of primary education back to parents and local authorities, while the government concentrates on secondary, technical and university education.

It is entirely right that the military régime should stamp out corruption in Nigerian public life, make corrupt politicians disgorge all their ill-gotten wealth, reorganize our public service, and produce a new constitution which will minimize regional and tribal conflicts; but one of its most vital tasks is to reorganize our educational system in such a way that educational development will keep pace with and encourage, economic growth. Indeed, unless it succeeds in the task of increasing employment opportunities and adapting the educational system to a predominantly agricultural economy, peaceful progress will be difficult to achieve.

The Head of the Military Government has repeatedly emphasized the overriding importance of national unity in the new order. All the study groups and working parties which he has set up so far have been directed to examine the different problems put to them in the context of national unity. But the concept of national unity goes deeper than a unified territorial state with political and economic centralization. It implies the integration of all our loyalties in one national symbol. In spite of the vast material improvements made since independence, we have so far failed to achieve an integrated loyalty; and because of this failure Nigerians, up to the end of the First Republic, were still arguing about political ends rather than about the means of achieving clearly defined and nationally accepted objectives. The disputes and hostilities which marred inter-regional cooperation were, deep down, not over means of achieving agreed national goals, like a higher standard of living for the masses, or a wider measure of individual liberty for all Nigerians, but over such issues as whether or not one Region ought to have a say in matters which another Region regarded as its domestic affair. In other words, the very existence of Nigeria as a single nation was still in doubt.

The contention that the affairs of Northern Nigeria were the exclusive concern of Northerners, and those of the East, Mid-West or West the responsibility only of those inhabiting these geographical areas; the belief that unity, peace and stability for the whole of Nigeria could be achieved only if each Region minded its own business; these were antithetical to national unity. National unity involves the pursuit of a common purpose by all groups in the country, be they political or religious. It implies the identification of the people with the nation-state. The greatest weakness of the First Republic was the existence of a multiplicity of purposes, some of which contradicted each other. The purpose of personal enrichment from public office was antithetical to the purpose of conferring the greatest good on the greatest number of citizens. Similarly, the purpose of entrenching tribal solidarity and privilege contradicted that of building a united nation. In spite of the high ideals set out in the preamble to our republican constitution, peace, social justice and individual liberty were not accepted as national goals. A structural reorganization of the constitution by itself will not produce a common national purpose, but it can facilitate a reorientation of the educational system towards common national goals. Before Nigeria achieved political independence, all political activity had a single purpose, the goal of national self-determination. There was a great deal of argument about the methods of reaching that goal; there was controversy about the timing and about the constitutional framework of independence; but the ultimate goal of independence was accepted by all the participants in the struggle. Since independence, there has not been one national purpose. If the revolution of 15 January 1966 succeeds in infusing a new national purpose in the people of Nigeria, then it will have been worth all the sacrifice it entailed.

Bibliographical Note

In the last five years several monographs studying in depth different aspects of modern Nigeria have been published in the United States and Europe. However, there are still very few general books about the country, and any reading list must, therefore, include as background material the older publications such as Lord Lugard's *Dual Mandate in Tropical Africa*, first published in 1922 and recently reissued by Frank Cass; William N. Geary's *Nigeria Under British Rule*, first published in 1934 and reprinted, also by Frank Cass, in 1966; Alan Burns, *A History of Nigeria* (Allen and Unwin, 1948); C. R. Niven, *Short History of Nigeria* (Longmans, Green, 1937); and Margery Perham, *Native Administration in Nigeria* (Oxford University Press, 1937).

More recent books on the history of Nigeria are J. F. A. Ajayi, *Milestones in Nigerian History* (Ibadan University Press, 1962) and M. Crowder, *The Story of Nigeria* (Faber, 1962), both of which are excellent general history.

Of the specialized monographs, the most outstanding are: K. O. Dike, *Trade and Politics in the Niger Delta (1830–1891)* (Oxford University Press, 1959) which describes the events leading to the establishment by Britain of a protectorate over that part of the country; J. F. A. Ajayi, *Christian Missions in Nigeria (1841–1891)* (Longmans, Green, 1965), an analysis of the educational and political influences of missionary activities; J. C. Anene, *Southern Nigeria in Transition (1885–1906)* (Cambridge University Press, 1965), a detailed discussion of the events leading to the establishment of a British Protectorate in Southern Nigeria.

Several books have appeared in recent years on constitutional development, but there is none more important than Obafemi Awolowo's *Path to Nigerian Freedom*, first published by Faber in

1947 and reprinted in 1966. Other publications on the subject are: K. Ezera, *Constitutional Developments in Nigeria* (Cambridge University Press, 1961); H. O. Davies, *Nigeria: The Prospects of Democracy* (Weidenfeld & Nicolson, 1961); O. I. Odumosu, *The Nigerian Constitution: Its History and Development* (Sweet and Maxwell, 1963).

Recent political development has been the subject of several scholarly investigations by American, European and Nigerian academics in recent years, and noteworthy publications on this subject include: R. D. Tilman and T. Cole, *The Nigerian Political Scene* (Duke University Press, 1962); Richard L. Sklar, *Nigerian Political Parties* (Princeton University Press, 1963); Hans N. Weiler, ed., *Erziehung und Politik in Nigeria/Education and Politics in Nigeria* (Verlag Rombach, Freiburg im Breisgau, 1964); T. N. Tamuno, *Nigeria and Elective Representation (1923–1947)* (Heinemann, 1966); J. P. Mackintosh, *Nigerian Government and Politics* (Allen and Unwin, 1966).

Two books of special interest published recently are Stanhope White, *Dan Bana* (Cassell, 1966), which is an account of the personal experience of an ex-District Officer in Northern Nigeria; and A. H. M. Kirk-Greene, *Principles of Native Administration in Nigeria* (Oxford University Press, 1965). Both present a perceptive picture of the practical problems of government at the local level in Northern Nigeria.

In the field of economics outstanding studies of the Colonial era are: A. N. Cook, *British Enterprise in Nigeria* (University of Philadelphia Press, 1943; reprinted by Frank Cass, 1963); Daryll Forde and Richendo Scott, *The Native Economics of Nigeria* (Faber, 1946); P. A. Bower, A. J. Brown *et al.*, *Mining Commerce and Finance in Nigeria* (Faber, 1948). More recent publications on the subject are: P. N. Okigbo, *Nigerian Public Finance* (Longmans of Nigeria, 1966), which deals mainly with the historical development of the principles of public finance applied in Nigeria; S. P. Schatz, *Development Bank Lending in Nigeria: The Federal Loans Board* (Oxford University Press, 1965); G. C. Onyemelukwe, *Problems of Industrial Planning and Management In Nigeria* (Longmans of Nigeria, 1966); C. V. Brown, *The Nigerian Banking System* (Allen and Unwin, 1966).

Several sociological studies of different Nigerian communities have been published in recent years. The following are a sample of the large number of excellent monographs on the culture and social organization of the different Nigerian peoples: C. E. Hopen, *The Pastoral Fulbe Family in Gwandu* (International African Institute, 1958); M. G. Smith, *Government in Zazzau, 1880–1950* (Oxford University Press for the International African Institute, 1960); G. I. Jones, *The Trading States of the Oil Rivers* (International African Institute, 1964); G. J. A. Ojo, *Yoruba Culture* (University of London Press, 1965); G. B. A. Coker, *Family Property among the Yoruba* (Sweet & Maxwell – African University Press, 1966); N. Okoro, *The Customary Laws of Succession in Eastern Nigeria* (Sweet & Maxwell – African University Press, 1966).

The International African Institute has published several volumes of summaries of scholarly monographs on Nigerian peoples in a series called the *Ethnographic Survey of Africa* edited by Professor Daryll Forde of London University. Included in the series are: Daryll Forde and G. I. Jones, *The Ibo and Ibibio-speaking Peoples of South-Eastern Nigeria*; Harold D. Gunn, *The Peoples of the Plateau Area of Northern Nigeria*; Daryll Forde and others, *Peoples of the Niger–Benue Confluence*; Laura and Paul Bohanan, *The Tiv of Central Nigeria*; Harold D. Gunn and F. P. Conant, *Peoples of the Middle Niger Region of Northern Nigeria*; R. E. Bradley, *The Benin Kingdom and the Edo-speaking Peoples of South-Western Nigeria*; Daryll Forde, *The Yoruba-speaking Peoples of South-Western Nigeria.*

Finally, the main theme of most of the creative writing by Nigerians about Nigeria is the problem of personal adjustment in a period of change from small-scale societies to modern complex communities. A few of the many outstanding works in this field are Chinua Achebe, *Things Fall Apart* (Heinemann, 1958), *No Longer at Ease* (Heinemann, 1960) and *A Man of the People* (Heinemann, 1966); Cyprian Ekwensi, *People of the City* (Heinemann, 1963) and *Jaguar Nana* (Panther Books, 1963); and Nkem Nwankwo, *Danda* (André Deutsch, 1964), all of which discuss the conflicts both individual and communal, between the traditional Nigerian cultures and the spreading Western culture.

References

Chapter 1

1 DARYLL FORDE: 'The Cultural Map of West Africa: Successive Adaptations to Tropical Forests and Grasslands', *Transactions of the New York Academy of Sciences*, series 2, vol. 15, pp. 206–19, April 1953

2 C. R. NIVEN: *A Short History of Nigeria*, ch. 3, Longmans, Green, 1937

3 DARYLL FORDE: op. cit.

4 OKOI ARIKPO: *Who are The Nigerians?* Lugard Lectures, 1957, Federal Ministry of Information, Lagos, 1958

5 S. O. BIOBAKU: *The Yoruba and Their Neighbours*, Lugard Lectures, 1956, Federal Ministry of Information, Lagos, 1958

6 *Population Census of Nigeria*, published by the Census Superintendent (Government Statistician), Lagos, 1953

7 ROBERT G. ARMSTRONG: 'The Igalla- and Idoma-Speaking Peoples' in Daryll Forde, P. Brown and R. C. Armstrong: *Peoples of the Niger–Benue Confluence*, Ethnographic Survey of Africa, International African Institute, London, 1955

Chapter 2

8 K. O. DIKE: *Trade and Politics in the Niger Delta (1830–1855)*, Oxford University Press, 1956

9 ELLEN THORP: *Ladder of Bones*, Jonathan Cape, 1956

10 K. O. DIKE: op. cit.

11 *Proceedings of the Legislative Council of Lagos, 6 May 1872*, National Archives Library, University of Ibadan

12 *Legislative Council of Lagos, 1886*, Government Printers, Lagos

13 SIR FREDERICK LUGARD: *Political Memorandum, 1913*, National Archives Library, University of Ibadan

Chapter 3

14 *Legislative Council Debates, 1918–1919*, Government Printer, Lagos

15 Sessional Paper no. 4 of 1945: *Political and Constitutional Future of Nigeria*, Government Printer, Lagos, 1945

16 *Laws of Nigeria*, 1948 edition, vol. 11, p. 18

Chapter 4

17 *Memorandum of the Case of the National Congress of British West Africa for a Memorial Based upon the Resolutions to be Presented to His Majesty the King Emperor in Council through the Right Honourable the Secretary of State for the Colonies* – London 1920

Chapter 5

18 *Legislative Council Debates 1948*, Government Printer, Lagos

19 *Legislative Council Debates 1948–1949*, Government Printer, Lagos, 1949

20 *Proceedings of the General Conference on the Review of the Constitution, January 1950*, pp. 239, 238, Government Printer, Lagos, 1950

21 Nigeria (Constitution) Order-in-Council, 1951, Section 107(2)

22 ibid., Section 118

23 *Eastern House of Assembly Debates; Second Session, vol. 2, 1953*, Government Printer, Nigeria, 1953

24 *House of Representatives Debates, March 1953*, Government Printer, Lagos, 1953

25 *Report on the Kano Disturbances of May 1953*, published under the authority of the Northern Regional Government, printed by the Government Printer, Nigeria, 1953

Chapter 6

26 OKOI ARIKPO: 'Future of Nigerian Federalism', *West Africa* no. 1996–2001, June–July 1956

27 K. C. WHEARE: The chapter 'Some Prerequisites of Federal Government' in *Federal Government*, Oxford University Press, 4th edition, 1963

28 CHIEF OBAFEMI AWOLOWO: *AWO: Autobiography of Chief Obafemi Awolowo*, Cambridge University Press, 1960

29 *Report of the Commission on Revenue Allocation*, J. R. Hicks and Sydney Phillipson, Government Printer, Lagos, 1951

Chapter 7

30 *Annual Digest of Educational Statistics*, series no. 1, vol. 3, 1963, Federal Ministry of Education, printed by the Nigerian National Press, Lagos

31 *Report on the Review of the Educational System in Eastern Nigeria* by Dr K. O. Dike and others, Official Document no. 19 of 1962, Government Printer, Enugu, 1962

32 *Investment in Education: The Report of the Commission on Post-School Certificate and Higher Education in Nigeria* (universally known as the Ashby Report), printed for the Commission by St Clements Press, London, 1960

33 *Nigeria's High-level Manpower* (1963–70), National Manpower Board Study no. 2, 1964, printed by the Nigerian National Press, Lagos

34 *University Development in Nigeria: Report of the National Universities Commission*, Federal Ministry of Information, 1963. The figures for the academic year, 1963–4 are taken from the Commission's *Annual Review of Nigerian Universities* for that Session

35 R. WRAITH AND E. SIMPKINS: *Corruption in Developing Countries*, Allen & Unwin, 1963

Chapter 8

36 Adegbenro v. Attorney-General of the Federation, Federal Supreme Court

37 *State House Diary*, published by the Federal Ministry of Information, Lagos, 1965

38 *Daily Times*, 12 November 1965, p. 9

39 *Daily Times*, 20 November 1965, pp. 1 and 6

40 *Daily Times*, 24 November 1965, p. 7

41 *Daily Times*, 24 November 1965, p. 7

42 *Daily Times*, 17 November 1965, p. 1

Index